PLACE, NOT RACE

PLACE,
not
RACE

A New Vision of
Opportunity in America

Sheryll Cashin

Beacon Press
Boston

BEACON PRESS
Boston, Massachusetts
www.beacon.org

Beacon Press books
are published under the auspices of
the Unitarian Universalist Association of Congregations.

17 16 15 14   8 7 6 5 4 3 2 1

This book is printed on acid-free paper that meets the uncoated paper
ANSI/NISO specifications for permanence as revised in 1992.

Text design and composition by Kim Arney

Library of Congress Cataloging-in-Publication Data
Cashin, Sheryll.
Place, not race : a new vision of opportunity in America / Sheryll Cashin.
pages   cm
Includes bibliographical references.
ISBN 978-0-8070-8614-8 (hardcover)
ISBN 978-0-8070-8615-5 (ebook)
1. Affirmative action programs in education—United States. 2. Discrimination
in education—Law and legislation—United States. 3. Universities and colleges—
United States—Admission. 4. Minorities—Education (Higher)—United States.
5. Educational equalization—United States. 6. Multicultural education—United
States. 7. Cultural pluralism—United States. I. Title.
LC213.52.C38 2014
370.117—dc23
2013048249

For Logan and Langston,
with faith that your generation will be better.

CONTENTS

Introduction ix

CHAPTER ONE
White Resentment, the Declining
Use of Race, and Gridlock 1

CHAPTER TWO
Place Matters 19

CHAPTER THREE
Optical Diversity vs. Real Inclusion 41

CHAPTER FOUR
Place, Not Race,
and Other Radical Reforms 63

CHAPTER FIVE
Reconciliation 89

Conclusion 109
Epilogue: A Letter to My Sons 113
Acknowledgments 121
Notes 125

INTRODUCTION

This book is about fairness. The US economy has become a pyramid in which nearly three-quarters of the jobs that will become available in this decade are predicted to pay a median wage of less than $35,000 a year and require only a high school diploma or less.[1] The so-called knowledge economy belongs to the few able to enter it, and the traditional gateway is selective higher education. I focus in this book on the structural barriers to accessing high-opportunity colleges for this reason. Fairness requires that their doors be open to all exceptional achievers, not just those who are already advantaged. The stratifications of K-12 education are mirrored in higher education, and in both systems the phenomenon of "opportunity hoarding" described by sociologist Charles Tilley seems to be at work.[2]

Those blessed to occupy golden neighborhoods and schools are most likely to enter equally golden colleges. Intentionally or not, they can block access by those outside their advantaged networks through in-group sanctioned practices like legacy preferences, "merit" aid, and the overuse of standardized test scores that track income status. Ironically, race-based affirmative action may also contribute to the hoarding phenomenon because advantaged racial minorities are most likely to benefit from the policy, and, as I argue, the optical diversity this creates undermines the possibility that elite colleges will rethink exclusionary practices.

In this book, I challenge universities to reform both affirmative action and the entire admissions process. But hoarding of selective education is only one strain of the unfairness that pervades America. My aim is to begin a larger conversation about how to create a politics of fairness that will help the vast majority of Americans who will not attend Harvard, Yale, or the University of Illinois.

A professional black woman describes to me her sister's fury when black children from low-income neighborhoods were given preferences to improve their access to sought-after magnet programs in Chicago public schools. The sister was angry when her middle-class black kids who did not live in the 'hood did not gain entrance, although they had better academic records. Is this what America has come to—a country where advantaged people of all colors look at growing inequality and are reduced to invoking numerical standards that block out others, and complaining when those others do gain access? Is this the country you want to live in, dear reader?

FAIRNESS IN COLLEGE ADMISSIONS

Abigail Fisher had a complaint that resonated with most Americans. The cherub-faced strawberry blond wanted her dream school, the University of Texas, to evaluate her and her competitors without any consideration of race. She did not want to be seen as a white girl from a suburb named Sugar Land, presumably the wrong race and place in a withering competition that has gone global. Nor did she think it fair that other applicants might benefit from having more melanin. "There were people in my class with lower grades who weren't in all the activities I was in, who were being accepted into UT, and the only difference between us was the color of our skin," she said in a YouTube video posted by her lawyers.[3]

Her argument is one we've heard before. Blacks and Latinos with lower test scores and grades than hers got in and that, she concluded, violated her right to equal protection under the Constitution. It didn't matter to Fisher or her lawyers that forty-two white applicants with lower numbers than hers were also admitted. They focused on the theoretical possibility that the five applicants of color with lower scores who gained entrance may have succeeded where Fisher failed, solely because of their race.[4]

Who knows for certain why Fisher did not emerge from ambiguity? Had she graduated in the top 10 percent of her high school class, she would have gained automatic entrance to the flagship university that both her father and sister attended. Instead she and other less stellar applicants had to compete head to head for the remaining 19 percent of slots in the UT Class of 2012. Her application probably landed in the "maybe" pile, its occupants neither obvious admits nor rejects. These are the applications conscientious admissions officers agonize over. A strong, authentic voice crying out from an absorbing personal essay or a soaring letter of recommendation that rings as true can make the difference.

In addition to high school rank and standardized test scores, UT considered personal achievement based upon two essays and factors like leadership, extracurricular activities, community service, work experience, socioeconomic status, and—the eternal bugaboo—race. Fisher's argument that race played a definitive role certainly resonates with how most white people feel about affirmative action in higher education. They think it is unfair to them and their children, and this explains why many institutions have been retreating from considering race in admissions.

The Supreme Court's 2013 compromise decision in *Fisher v. Texas* extended the life of race-based affirmative action. But there will always be another Abigail Fisher. When a disgruntled applicant sues, defenders of an affirmative action policy must convince the court that there are "no workable race-neutral alternatives" to achieve the educational benefits of diversity. Conservatives will continue to attack the policy in courts and through politics. With one exception, every time the issue of affirmative action has been placed on a state ballot, voters have banned the policy. As this book went to print, the Supreme Court had heard argument but not issued a decision in the case of *Schuette v. Coalition to Defend Affirmative Action,* in which the ability of Michigan voters to ban affirmative action is challenged. At oral argument, conservative justices seemed inclined to uphold the ban. However the court rules, political opposition to use of race in college admissions will continue.

This is particularly easy politics for Republicans. On the day Barack Obama was re-elected president, voters in Oklahoma approved an amendment to their state constitution to prohibit affirmative action based upon race, gender, ethnicity or national origin in public employment, education, and contracting.[5] At the time this was the third ban successfully sponsored by Republican state legislators in three years. They no longer needed a black man, Ward Connerly, for cover. Political mobilization against affirmative action accords with the mood of a browning country in which white guys increasingly feel victimized. White anxiety about changing demographics shows up in online comments like one by "Andrew," who identified himself as living in the South. Opining on a *New York Times* story about California universities that had responded to a state ban on racial preferences by spending as much as $85 million on outreach and mentoring to expand the pipeline of college-ready applicants of color, Andrew wrote:

> *Diversity* = fewer white people, even in places where white people are already a minority, both in terms of their representation in the general population and their presence on campuses. If judges ban affirmative action, the ideologues who run our institutions of higher education will simply ignore the law and proclaim "holistic admission practices" in order to decrease the number of white students admitted, much as they have done in California, Michigan and elsewhere in recent years.

His was among the most recommended comments on the story, presumably because it resonated with many white readers. White anxiety will continue to rise as more whites become minorities in their states or communities. Institutions necessarily are changing to accommodate domestic demographic change and globalization. The future is Rice University: today, at this preeminent school founded on a "whites-only" charter, less than half of the undergraduates are white Americans.[6] At Rice, native students of color and international students are taking places that literally were once reserved for white people, and some whites are not dealing well with such transitions.

THE PERCEPTION GAP

A student of mine testifies to the angst whites share with him because he is a member of that club—honest tribal talk that I will only hear if a race traitor like my student shares it with me. My student—I will call him Ted—tells me about a former Dalton School classmate who was livid when his four-year-old did not get into their alma mater's pre-K class, half of which was now populated by the rainbow. Dalton is an elite prep school on New York's Upper East Side with a reputation for progressivism that decided in 2007 to make diversity "an integral part of school life," according to its mission statement. By 2011, the numbers of non-white kindergarteners went from 6 percent to 47 percent of the entering class, with predictable commentary from disappointed parents on UrbanBaby.com.[7] "*They* took my kid's spot!" Ted's ostensibly liberal, shut-out former classmate exclaimed. Even one-percenters are forced to adapt. As Ted relates the story to me, he titters with nervous laughter and recognition. When friends or strangers raise this complaint, should he question their underlying assumptions of entitlement and superiority, or just let them vent?

Such gripes, and worse, are easy to find online. Just read the comments to any news story about affirmative action. Jonica Witherspoon, a graduate of Northwestern, confessed to a reporter in the *Chicago Sun-Times* that given her scores on standardized tests, she "probably wouldn't have made the cut to attend Northwestern" if she were not African American. She did not begrudge affluent Jamaicans and Nigerians, "who may have taken a spot that would have gone to somebody from, say, Chicago's West Side." "It's good for you," she said. "You see these successful, smart people out there who are black and you think, 'Maybe I can be one of them. Maybe I can do better.'"[8] An online commenter identified as Razz Barry felt differently: "I resent her taking the place of some white man, with higher test scores, who may have discovered a cure for cancer, invented a fuel to end our dependency on Arab oil . . ." He trailed off.

Barry's suggestion that affirmative action squelches opportunity for would-be white heroes overlooks the fact that Superman leaps over obstacles. Were he rejected by Northwestern, most likely Clark Kent would be accepted and thrive elsewhere. Abigail Fisher declined an offer to attend a different Texas institution, with a possibility of later transferring to UT. Instead she sued, leaving her case to activist lawyers and heading off to Louisiana State University, where she graduated with a degree in finance in 2012. Through her own resilience and determination, her life did not grind to a halt. That said, many people feel her pain.

In a 2012 Rasmussen poll, 55 percent of respondents opposed affirmative action in college admissions.[9] In a 2009 Quinnipiac University poll of registered voters, 55 percent said affirmative action should be abolished.[10] Although proponents of affirmative action argue that such programs advance only qualified minorities and don't disadvantage others, as the Quinnipiac pollsters put it, "voters see a zero-sum game in which someone—generally white males—loses when someone else gains."[11] For the white parent who fills Adderall prescriptions for a teenager for whom "above average" is not good enough, observing Cosby kids advance is a provocation.

Although legions of non-blacks and women have benefited from affirmative action, inconveniently for its proponents, the policy has a black face and remains a dog whistle for political mobilization. It is hard for non-blacks to see blacks as disadvantaged and needing affirmative action when examples of black success are ubiquitous, from Obama to Oprah to Jay-Z, not to mention black bosses non-blacks may report to, fictional black surgeons and lawyers they encounter on TV, and well-dressed black people driving expensive cars they occasionally notice on their daily commute. Americans are also now regularly offered steamy examples of interracial romance on small and large screens. Even a dark-skinned brother is now allowed to seduce a pale woman, the ultimate suggestion of black equality.

While non-blacks see real and virtual examples of black success every day, they don't see black poverty, because they are removed from the deprivations of ghetto neighborhoods. Not surprisingly, only 49 percent of participants in a 2009 Pew survey believed that African Americans were subject to "a lot of discrimination." A majority of survey participants did perceive *other* groups as enduring serious discrimination: Latinos (52 percent), Muslims (58 percent), and gays and lesbians (64 percent).[12]

African Americans have arrived, in the minds of many non-blacks. In a 2007 Pew survey of racial attitudes, 84 percent of participants had a favorable view of African Americans, while only 10 percent expressed an unfavorable view of them.[13] Since Barack Obama was elected president, however, more people express explicitly anti-black views.[14] And a large body of research by social psychologists demonstrates that most people harbor subconscious biases about black people.[15] Americans remain complicated about race. We are at war with ourselves inside our heads. Despite biases against "the other," the vast majority of all Americans view racial discrimination as wrong, even un-American, and self-identify as anti-racist. Their anti-racist identity coupled with ubiquitous examples of black success likely inform their judgment that affirmative action is unfair and no longer necessary.

In opinion polls, African Americans register the strongest support for affirmative action. This is not hard to understand. Those on the receiving end of real or perceived racial discrimination—from taxis that pass them by to security guards who trail them in clothing stores to bad schools or incarcerated family members—also harbor a sense of grievance. The civil rights revolution is not over yet. Watching Obama on TV and the race pride that engenders does not make up for twice the unemployment, nearly three times the poverty, and six times the incarceration that white people endure.[16] In the consciously black mind, history and present-day inequalities are frontal. Black folks live with a constant awareness of the myriad ways in which race can obstruct, interfere, or in nightmarish, Trayvon-esque scenarios, ruin one's life. For many African Americans, affirmative action is a modest palliative, but a fair one, given the systemic forces black people endured historically and continue to face.

As I describe in this book, these gaps of perception about race undermine possibilities for opponents and proponents of affirmative action to join forces to make systems of education and opportunity better and more responsive to everyone. To borrow an apt phrase from a self-described "gun guy" who seeks common ground between his gun-toting brothers and gun-control advocates who may be clueless or dismissive about the culture of huntsmen, "there is no tree for these folks to gather under."[17] On the issue of affirmative action, there are no forums for addressing common concerns, or even building a sense of the common good. The civil rights tent is not viewed as a place where the concerns of struggling whites will be heard. Movement conservatives allied against affirmative action are viewed with suspicion by many people of color. This perception gap puts universities that are serious about diversity in a quandary. Going forward, should they still try to use race and risk lawsuits from disappointed white applicants? Or risk the ire of Republican state legislators who have picked up the movement Ward Connelly began?

I prefer place, rather than race, as the focus of affirmative action for the pragmatic reason that it will foster more social cohesion and a better politics. More importantly, it will help those *actually* disadvantaged by segregation. Those who suffer the deprivations of high-poverty neighborhoods and schools are deserving of special consideration. Those blessed to come of age in poverty-free havens are not. Race still matters in American society, particularly in the criminal justice system. But race is under-inclusive. As Walter Benn Michaels, professor at the University of Illinois, bluntly put it to the *Journal of Blacks in Higher Education:* "When students and faculty activists struggle for cultural diversity, they are in large part battling over what skin color the rich kids have."[18]

As I will show in subsequent chapters, race does not, by definition, capture those who suffer the structural disadvantages of segregated schools and neighborhoods. Race is also over-inclusive in that it can capture people with dark skin who are exceedingly advantaged. African immigrants, on average, are better educated than *every* American subgroup, including Asians and whites. The mantra of diversity might be applied to a school that admits African elites or their American cousins, like Sasha, Malia, Blue Ivy, or my kids. But diversity by phenotype puts no pressure on institutions to dismantle underlying systems of exclusion that propagate inequality.

When President Lyndon Johnson framed the argument for affirmative action at a commencement address at Howard University in 1965, the Civil Rights Act of 1964 was an infant. The antidiscrimination principle the act embodied, so widely embraced today, was also new and meeting resistance. About half of blacks, still "Negroes" at the time, lived below the poverty line. The black middle class was beginning to emerge. A two-parent black professional family, for example a teacher and an equal employment opportunity officer at IBM, would likely have been trained at historically black institutions and needed a lift to gain entry into predominately white ones. Centuries of exclusionary habits didn't die easily; affirmative efforts were needed, Johnson argued. "This is the next and more profound stage of the battle for civil rights," he intoned. "We seek not just freedom . . . but equality as a fact and as a result."[19]

Back then, race and gender were appropriate markers for the type of exclusion practiced by most predominately white universities. Today, place is a more appropriate indicator of who gets excluded from consideration by admissions officers at selective institutions. Every high school in America has a cadre of strivers. Diversity by skin color enables universities to bypass achievers from inner-city, rural, and struggling suburban environs—kids who weren't handed perfection but did their very best with what they had. Phenotypic diversity also assuages what is left of white guilt and helps mask exclusion. Affluent people of all colors who call an SAT score merit are complicit in this.

THE PROMISE OF *BROWN V. BOARD OF EDUCATION*

In 1954, the Supreme Court determined that segregated public education deprived "children of the minority group" of equal educational opportunity. Six decades later, public education remains largely segregated. As we celebrate or distance ourselves from the latest decennial anniversary of the Supreme Court's decision in *Brown v. Board of Education,* we must contend with the reality that high-quality K-12 education is not widely distributed. The discourse in America about segregation is dishonest. On the surface, we pretend that the values of *Brown v. Board of Education* have been met, although most of us know in our hearts that public education usually betrays those values.

This result was not inevitable. As a post–civil rights baby, I attended integrated public schools in Alabama during the era when the state and nation were making good on the promise of *Brown v. Board of Education.* I graduated from S. R. Butler High School in Huntsville in 1980. At the time it was one of the largest schools in the state. Our mascot was the Butler Rebel, a confederate colonel who appeared more avuncular than defiant. Butler was an integrated but majority-white powerhouse in sports and a place where a nerd like me could take Advanced Placement classes and gain entrance to great colleges. Kids from housing projects and sturdy, middle-class neighborhoods attended the same school, albeit with a degree of sorting into racially identifiable academic tracks. We played on sports fields together, attended the same "fifth quarter" dances, and generally got along.

At our thirtieth reunion, my classmates and I bemoaned Butler's demise. Enrollment at the school we had thrived at and loved had dwindled to 35 percent of capacity, depleted by demographic change. It had become an impoverished, predominately black, low-opportunity school and the object of derision, despite its string of state basketball championships in the 2000s. Barely half of its seniors graduated, and its students *were* being "left behind" as families with options moved on and standardized test scores declined. Middle-class people exited the neighborhoods surrounding the school, opting for greener, higher-opportunity acres in rapidly growing suburban Madison County. The state accelerated the school's isolation when it built an interstate highway connector that mowed down scores of homes in Butler's attendance zone. As in most other cities where links to the interstate were laid decades before, this created a concrete firewall between the majority-white, affluent and majority-black, declining sides of town, with predictable results for our alma mater. A similar story of race and class segregation could be told in most American cities with a critical mass of people of color.

I feel blessed to have come of age in the 1970s, when there was still much opportunity to live a middle-class life. Despite being the child of broke activists who paid dearly for challenging Alabama-style apartheid, my high-quality, free public education set me on an extraordinary path. As a co-valedictorian from Butler I was able to enter Vanderbilt University on an honors scholarship and found that, despite an SAT score that was solid but not stratospheric, Butler had prepared me to compete. I chose to study engineering because Wernher von Braun had made rocket science a common occupation in Huntsville and it was an easy route to scholarships and financial security for a black girl who got As in physics and trigonometry.

Vanderbilt became my financial parent, as did the British government when I parlayed a summa degree in electrical engineering into a Marshall Scholarship to study law at Oxford University. I recall writing a letter from Oxford to my AP English teacher at Butler, Mrs. Calloway, thanking her for teaching me how to compose a coherent essay. As I endured the trauma of the British approach to finals—eight closed-book exams in eight days covering two years of material—I was steadied by the fundamentals of good writing that I learned from this gifted, passionate public school teacher. I went on to graduate from Harvard Law School and to work as a law clerk for Justice Thurgood Marshall, the chief oral advocate for *Brown* who had done so much to make my trajectory possible.

As my generation of post–civil rights era babies was integrating schools and preparing for life, politicians started culture wars, a war on drugs, and a cynical politics of racial resentment. And our nation retreated from the promise of *Brown*. Ten years ago, in marking the fiftieth anniversary of the decision, I wrote a book with the happy title *The Failures of Integration* arguing that the only route to true equality was the hardest one, integration. Since then racial segregation in neighborhoods has continued to decline modestly, even as the affluent have become more separated from everyone else. As a result, place—where one lives—powerfully structures opportunity. Exclusion from the good life, good schools and jobs, and middle class stability is no longer based primarily on race, as was the case in the Jim Crow era. While race certainly plays a role in the geographic sorting that goes on in residential housing markets, it is no longer a definitive marker for who is disadvantaged, because a person of color who has the means can escape admittedly racialized segregation. Meanwhile, for those of any color relegated to low-opportunity environs, geography is largely destiny.

In this book I reflect on how twenty-first century segregation contributes to the achievement gap that has made race-based affirmative action necessary. Less than one-third of black and Latino children live in middle-class neighborhoods; exposure to extensive poverty is the norm for most of them, while the opposite is true for most white and Asian children. That said, not all white and Asian children are privileged, and not all black and Latino children are poor.

MORAL CLARITY

The rub for proponents of affirmative action is that as long as they hold on to race as the sine qua non of diversity, they stymie possibilities for transformative change. The civil rights community, for example, expends energy on a policy that primarily benefits the most advantaged children of color, while contributing to a divisive politics that makes it difficult to create quality K-12 education for all children. I argue that the next generation of diversity strategies should encourage rather than discourage cross-racial alliances and social mobility. I contend that meaningful diversity can be achieved if institutions rethink exclusionary practices, cultivate strivers from overlooked places, and give special consideration to highly qualified applicants of all races that have had to overcome structural disadvantages like segregation. I call it "diversity practice" because we need to jettison the label affirmative action, with its loaded meanings, and create new, fairer structures of opportunity through daily effort. The goal, over time, is to create a society where getting ahead is not a function of circumstances of birth.

That august task will require a more cohesive politics, and any winning majority necessarily will be multiracial. Our present collective goal must be the same one Dr. Martin Luther King Jr. articulated at the dawn of the civil rights movement. In championing nonviolence as the means to dismantling Jim Crow, King always reminded his audience of his ultimate vision for America. "[T]he end is reconciliation; the end is redemption," he said, and "the creation of the beloved community." To "make it possible for men to live together as brothers in a community, and not continually live with bitterness and friction"—that was King's end, and the unfinished work to which each generation of Americans must be dedicated.[20]

The moral authority that flowed from John Lewis and others volunteering to get their heads beat in on the Edmund Pettus Bridge did much to render the movement "everybody's fight"—the words Viola Liuzzo used to justify leaving her five children in Michigan to join with civil rights activists in Alabama. King saw in the Freedom Riders and his increasingly multiracial band of civil rights soldiers an early example of the beloved community he espoused. The movement itself could be an approximation of the spirit of agape love and community that he envisioned for the whole of America. One expression of this love for community was seeing the mutuality in all types of human suffering. As King famously said, "Injustice anywhere is a threat to justice everywhere."[21] In the end, he did not turn away from the hardest part of community building. In his last book, King wrote, "Our loyalties must transcend our race, our tribe, our class, and our nation."[22]

There are obvious lessons here for proponents of diversity. Race-based affirmative action buys some diversity for a relative few, but not serious inclusion. It doesn't help to build a movement to attack underlying systems of inequality that are eating away at the soul of our nation. Among other transformations, we need corporations that share more profits with workers and pay them equitably. We need a financial system that doesn't exploit average people. We need governments that invest wisely in pre–K-12 education and the nonselective higher education that at least half of high school graduates attend. We also need government that does not over-incarcerate high school dropouts of all colors.[23]

The means of race pushes away potential allies in a way that makes it mathematically impossible to build multiracial alliances for sanity and common sense. Throughout this book, I draw on social science research to explain how race can and cannot be used effectively to build cross-racial alliances. In the context of promoting diversity on college campuses, place is a better mechanism that will also encourage alliances among those mutually excluded by current systems. Ultimately, I argue that, given our nation's failure to live up to *Brown,* we have an obligation to acknowledge and ameliorate the injustices of segregation—a moral imperative more important than diversity itself. The idea of America will only become true when those who suffer mutual oppressions unite to create real opportunity for everyone.

CHAPTER ONE

White Resentment, the Declining Use of Race, and Gridlock

Berkeley College Republicans will be SELLING BAKED GOODS from 10 AM–2PM across from the Affirmative Action Phonebank on Upper Sproul, and just like the CA Senate Bills 185 and 387 the phonebank supports, we will be considering RACE, GENDER, ETHNICITY, NATIONAL/GEOGRAPHIC ORIGIN and other relevant factors to ensure the EQUITABLE distribution of BAKED GOODS to our DIVERSE! student body. To ensure the fairest distribution, and make sure that there are a DIVERSE population of RACES of students getting BCR's delicious baked goods, the pricing structure will be as follows:

> *White/Caucasian: $2.00*
> *Asian/Asian American: $1.50*
> *Latino/Hispanic: $1.00*
> *Black/African American: $0.75*
> *Native American: $0.25*
> *$0.25 OFF FOR ALL WOMEN!*

Hope to see you all there! If you don't come, you're a racist!

This Facebook event caused a stir on the University of California-Berkeley campus. Countercharges of racism flew. The Berkeley College Republicans who conceived it as a protest to proposed legislation to reintroduce some race consciousness into UC admissions responded to the torrent of negative criticism and some threats with this polite clarification: "The pricing structure of the baked goods is meant to be satirical, while urging students to think more critically about the implications of this policy."[1] On the day of the event, cameras rolled and national reporters hovered, catching exchanges between the aggrieved and the more aggrieved. A white woman bought a cupcake to show solidarity with the premise of the protest. The Black Student Union staged a counterprotest that received much less press attention.[2] They wore all-black clothes and laid their black bodies end to end on the concrete, a symbolic image as open to individual interpretation as the bake sale itself. Similar bake sales have been mounted at dozens of other campuses across the country.

Ultimately Governor Jerry Brown vetoed the proposed legislation, which would have overturned the Proposition 209 ban on affirmative action, as had his predecessor, Arnold Schwarzenegger. Brown said that he agreed "wholeheartedly" with the goal of the bill, but he conceded to the constraints of law and, implicitly, of politics. If he signed the bill, opponents would sue, claiming it violated the will of the voters who approved Prop 209 to ban affirmative action in 1996. Rather than waste time and confusion on lawsuits about the legislation, he left it to universities to test the limits of Prop 209 and the courts to police those limits. The president of the Berkeley College Republicans was sanguine after Brown's veto. He cited a Survey USA poll showing that 77 percent of Californians opposed the bill and applauded Brown for "respect[ing] the will of the voters." "The people of California believe, as does [*sic*] the Berkeley College Republicans, that college admission decisions should be based on the qualifications of the applicant and the individual challenges he or she has faced, not based on his or her race," he concluded.[3]

And so it goes in majority-minority California. Later I'll examine what the Golden State has done to create diversity on college campuses without using race, but here I argue that law and politics work against the use of race in the rest of the nation. Eight states have banned affirmative action programs, six through ballot measures (California, Washington, Michigan, Nebraska, Arizona, and Oklahoma), one by executive order (Florida), and another by legislative act (New Hampshire). However you may feel about the bake sales, the sentiments that motivated them are widely held and not going away. Most whites oppose affirmative action in college admissions even if they are not that demonstrative in public.

White resentment colors our politics, especially post-Obama. It is destined to grow as the country browns.

THE CONSTRAINTS OF LAW

Ideologically conservative members of the Supreme Court have embraced a color-blind constitutionalism that, as Justice Scalia put it, requires the Constitution to "focus upon the individual, and . . . [reject] dispositions based on race, . . . or based on blood."[4] The three white men and one "brother" to the right of Justice Kennedy on the Court belong to a league of aspiration. Chief Justice Roberts seems perplexed as to why we can't just move on. "The way to stop discrimination on the basis of race is to stop discriminating on the basis of race," he intoned in another case.[5] Complete color-blindness is a strange thing to wish for. The idea that we are not supposed to notice differences, even to celebrate them, seems artificial and sterile. Those who claim not to see color are probably lying to themselves. I don't believe the archconservatives on the Court mean it literally. For them color-blindness is a legal, not social, requirement.

I doubt that Chief Justice Roberts was color-blind when he adopted his children. I don't begrudge his choice to marry and parent within his race, as I have done. My point is that only the most ardent of integrators—perhaps Justice Thomas, who married interracially—is truly color-blind. The founders of this nation certainly were not. They embedded race and gender hierarchy into the text of our constitution and laws. The idea that there was ever any original constitutional position of color-blindness is a fiction, a convenient artifice introduced only after civil rights revolutionaries like Thurgood Marshall began to demand redress for racial wrongs. Color-blindness is not the inevitable or only reading of the words "equal protection of the laws." It is one thing to recommend, for pragmatic policy reasons, that we use nonracial means to create real inclusion on college campuses, as I do later in this book. It is quite another to contend, wrongly, that our constitution inherently demands color-blindness.[6]

Justice Kennedy is more receptive to the continued salience of race, but just a touch. Formal color-blindness—an absolute prohibition against consideration of race by the state—is not the supreme law of the land because Kennedy has withheld a fifth vote to make it so. But in practical terms, the Court does not distinguish between invidious uses of race—Jim Crow forms of exclusion—and modern attempts to include underrepresented minorities through affirmative action. Since its 1995 ruling in *Adarand Constructors v. Pena*, any use of race by the state will invoke the strictest of scrutiny under Fourteenth Amendment equal-protection analysis.[7]

The Court's 2003 decision in *Grutter v. Bollinger,* in which it upheld the University of Michigan Law School's holistic affirmative action program, was a rare example of a state's use of race surviving strict scrutiny. Justice O'Connor, author of the *Grutter* majority opinion, injected a degree of realism into equal-protection analysis. She deferred to universities, conceding that they had a compelling interest in diversity in higher education and according them discretion to use race as one flexible factor among several as a means to achieving that end. O'Connor's speculation that affirmative action might no longer be necessary a quarter-century later was actually a call to action. America was on notice that it had better get to work closing racial gaps of achievement, because use of race by the state would be time-limited.

With O'Connor's retirement and replacement by Justice Alito, also an adherent of color-blind constitutionalism, proponents of affirmative action have depended on Justice Kennedy for whatever shreds of the policy he may leave intact. That reliance is precarious. Kennedy dissented in *Grutter.* He has never voted to uphold an affirmative action program. Whether the issue is affirmative action, school integration, employment discrimination or some other context touching upon race, he has sounded a consistent theme. For him consideration of the race *of individuals* is not only unconstitutional but inherently demeaning. In *Rice v. Cayetano*, a case involving voting rights of non-native Hawaiians for election of public trustees of a fund to assist native Hawaiians, he stated: "One of the principal reasons race is treated as a forbidden classification is that it demeans the dignity and worth of a person to be judged by ancestry instead of by his or her own merit and essential qualities."

In his dissenting opinion in *Grutter,* Kennedy agreed with the majority that universities have a compelling interest in a diverse student body and stated, "There is no constitutional objection to the goal of considering race as one modest factor among many to achieve diversity." But, he reasoned, strict scrutiny required that universities deploy "sufficient procedures" to ensure each applicant receives individual consideration and that race does not become a predominant factor in admissions decisions. In Kennedy's view, the concept of critical mass deployed by Michigan's School of Law operated as a quota whereby race became determinative for those students left to compete for the final 15–20 percent of places offered to the entering class.

In *Fisher,* Justice Kennedy seemed to have made his peace with the *Grutter* decision by putting his gloss on it. Writing for the majority, he reaffirmed that universities have a compelling interest in the educational benefits of diversity and that they deserve deference on why diversity produces those benefits. Kennedy made it clear, however, that any use of race must be "narrowly tailored" and that judges, not universities, must decide that question. Kennedy clarified the standard for narrow tailoring as essentially a presumption against the use of race. When an affirmative action plan is challenged in court, the court must be satisfied that there are "no workable race-neutral alternatives" to achieve the educational benefits of diversity. In theory, a race-based affirmative action plan can survive strict scrutiny. But the Court imposed an exacting standard for narrow tailoring that will be difficult to meet. With each passing year, as demographic change and experimentation enhance possibilities for achieving diversity without using race, the challenge of surviving lawsuits filed by disgruntled applicants will grow more onerous.

Of course, the Supreme Court's gutting of a key provision of the Voting Rights Act the day after its decision in *Fisher* was the headline story about the Court and race as it concluded a contentious term in 2013. That and the divergence of opinion about George Zimmerman and Trayvon Martin, fights over immigration reform, and threats to bring the federal government to a standstill over Obamacare rounded out another summer of our discontent. The Voting Rights Act case, which freed Shelby County, Alabama, and other jurisdictions mainly in the former Confederacy from having to seek "preclearance" from the federal government for election law changes, was a more overt ode to color-blindness than the *Fisher* decision. As Justice Ginsberg wrote in her dissent, the majority did not deign to engage with a 15,000-page legislative record demonstrating pervasive, intentional racial discrimination by covered jurisdictions, especially in Alabama. The petite woman from the left accused the majority of "hubris" in blithely pointing to the fact of parity in voter registration and turnout among blacks and whites while turning a color-blind eye to massive evidence of continued discrimination against voters of color.[8] Abigail Fisher and Shelby County were recruited to sue and bankrolled by the same conservative legal defense fund, one devoted exclusively to challenging racial and ethnic classifications in state and federal courts. "For the next few years," according to the fund's website, it "will devote all of its efforts to influencing jurisprudence, public policy, and public attitudes regarding race and ethnicity."[9]

Race-based affirmative action had been declining in university admissions even before Abigail Fisher's case arrived at the Court. Since Ward Connerly kick-started a state-by-state political mobilization against affirmative action in the mid-1990s, the percentage of public four-year colleges that consider racial or ethnic status in admissions has fallen from about 60 percent to 35 percent. Only 45 percent of private colleges still explicitly consider race, with elite schools more likely to do so, although they, too, have retreated.[10]

THE CONSTRAINTS OF POLITICS

Race-based affirmative action is also increasingly untenable because of politics. While a majority of Americans say in opinion polls that they support affirmative action programs generally, when asked if they support racial considerations in college admissions, large majorities oppose. A June 2013 ABC/Washington Post poll posed this question: "Overall, do you support or oppose allowing universities to consider an applicant's race as a factor in deciding which students to admit?" Of those who responded, 76 percent opposed, 22 percent supported, and only 2 percent were undecided.[11]

In a 2013 poll conducted by the Public Religion Research Institute, while two-thirds of respondents favored affirmative action generally, 64 percent of respondents opposed racial preferences in college admissions, including a majority of Republicans (80 percent), independents (67 percent), and Democrats (53 percent). African Americans were the only subgroup that clearly favored consideration of race in admissions; Latinos were mixed, and the vast majority of whites were opposed. In a Pew

Research Center values survey released in 2009, only 31 percent agreed that "we should make every effort to improve the position of blacks and minorities, even if it means giving them preferential treatment," while 65 percent disagreed—a balance of opinion that has endured throughout most of the two-decade history of the Pew values survey. After the Great Recession, less than half of millennials supported this statement.[12]

Opponents of affirmative action have succeeded in harnessing such public opinion. With the exception of a proposed constitutional ban that was narrowly defeated in Colorado, whenever the issue of banning affirmative action has been placed before state voters, they have voted to end it. The three most recent state initiatives against affirmative action have been the work of Republican legislators. They have taken up the movement Ward Connerly started, bypassing the need for expensive ballot initiatives in states where they dominate. In Arizona and Oklahoma, GOP legislators successfully proposed constitutional bans put before the voters for approval. In New Hampshire, after Republicans gained control of both chambers of the legislature in 2010, a measure was introduced to prevent the state's university and community college system and all state agencies from considering "race, sex, national origin, religion, or sexual orientation" in recruiting, hiring, promotion, or admissions. It passed overwhelmingly in both houses and became law when the Democratic governor, John Lynch, took no action on it.

Opposing affirmative action has been a venerable plank in Republican politics for three decades. While affirmative action has eroded in popularity and usage at public and private institutions, what most endures about the policy is a political realignment, achieved by the GOP in the 1980s and 1990s, through a cynical wedge politics of racial resentment. Ronald Reagan ran for president in 1980 on a GOP platform that labeled affirmative action's goals and timetables as inherently discriminatory quotas. His coded appeals around a cluster of race-oriented issues resonated in the South and white ethnic suburbs of the Midwest and Northeast, swelling the ranks of "Reagan Democrats." Soon the GOP began to emerge as the "white party" and the Democrats as the "black party" among these voters. Such identification created no incentive for racial reconciliation, and great incentive for Republicans to create political majorities by dividing whites from blacks and people of color.

Ultimately, Reagan's main vehicle for undermining affirmative action was to gut enforcement. He cut funding for the Equal Employment Opportunity Commission (EEOC) and the civil rights division, and by 1984 the EEOC was filing 60 percent fewer cases than it did at the onset of his first term. Civil rights cases against segregation in schools or housing that traditionally had been filed by the Justice Department virtually disappeared by 1984. Reagan also replaced proponents of affirmative action on the Civil Rights Commission with vigorous opponents. Opposition to affirmative action and black-associated civil rights became a key aspect of the Reagan zeitgeist.

Subsequent Republican candidates from Jesse Helms to George H. W. Bush would also use racial wedge issues—affirmative action, busing, crime, capital punishment, Willie Horton—to make inroads with white working-class voters who had been dependable Democrats from 1932 to 1960. The stagflation of the 1970s and economic restructuring of the 1980s fueled these voters' resentments about race. In some blue-collar areas, race seemed to be *the* predominant factor in whites' transition from the Democratic to the Republican column. Macomb County, Michigan, just north of Detroit, offers a potent example. It went from being the most Democratic suburban county in the country in 1960, voting 63 percent for Kennedy that year, to voting 66 percent for Reagan in 1984. In focus groups, Democratic pollster Stanley Greenberg found racial resentment animated much of the switch:

> Blacks constitute the explanation for their vulnerability for almost everything that has gone wrong in their lives. [They see] the federal government "as a black domain where whites cannot expect reasonable treatment." . . . There was widespread sentiment . . . that the Democratic party supported giveaway programs, that is, programs aimed primarily at minorities.[13]

Fortunately, race-coded appeals now seem more likely to backfire than resonate with the American electorate. You can't yell "Macaca" at a crowded campaign rally or rail against welfare for "blah people" and succeed in getting yourself elected in a largely tolerant, multihued nation. But the overtly race-coded politics of a bygone era did break up the multiracial coalition that made the New Deal and civil rights possible. The New Deal model of politics pitted a winning coalition of economically marginal black and white Democrats against a small minority of wealthy Republicans. That model was replaced by a modern Republican Party that managed to unite many affluent, middle- and working-class white voters. In the 2012 presidential election, 58 percent of whites voted Republican, up from 55 percent in 2008 and equal to the 58 percent of whites who voted for George W. Bush in 2004. This is significantly higher than the GOP's share of the white vote in past presidential elections: 54 percent in 2000, 46 percent in 1996, and 40 percent in 1992.

The racial divide is even sharper among men. In 2012, 62 percent of white men voted for Mitt Romney, while men of color heavily favored Barack Obama (black men, 87 percent; Latino men, 65 percent; all other races, 66 percent).[14] Despite widespread talk of our black president ushering in a post-racial era, in the 2012 election the GOP gained significant percentages with every subcategory of white voter, including women and millennials.[15] Republicans gained the most ground with whites making $30,000–$75,000 annually.[16] The GOP also made great inroads with whites without a college degree. The only white economic subgroup that Obama won was whites making less than $30,000.[17]

THE PERCEPTION GAP: WHITE RESENTMENT IN THE AGE OF OBAMA

There is a perception gap in the electorate between blacks and non-blacks about affirmative action in college admissions and between whites and non-whites about issues of racial inequality generally. For example, a CNN survey conducted in 2009 found that 55 percent of blacks thought discrimination was a very serious problem, while only 17 percent of whites felt that way.[18] Similarly, according to a 2009 Pew Research Center survey on race, 80 percent of blacks felt that equality has not been achieved and 43 percent of blacks thought there was still "a lot of discrimination," while only 13 percent of whites believed that there was much anti-black bias.[19] The same survey also found that 54 percent of whites believed the country had made the necessary changes to give African Americans rights equal to whites, while only 13 percent of blacks believed this. Hispanic survey participants were divided on this question, with 42 percent saying they agreed the country had made the necessary changes to give blacks equal rights and 47 percent concluding that more changes were necessary.[20]

One psychology study suggests that whites and people of color have different perceptions about the extent of racial equality because they have different frames of reference. Arguably, whites have higher assessments of racial progress because they tend to compare the present to our Jim Crow past. People of color tend to compare the present to a future ideal of full equality.[21] In fact, *whites are more apt to perceive discrimination against themselves than against racial minorities.* A recent study found that all Americans think significant progress has been made against anti-black bias. But whites perceived that progress as coming at their expense, and they viewed anti-white bias as a bigger social problem than anti-black bias.[22]

Working-class whites are in a serious funk. They are more pessimistic about their future prospects than are blacks and Latinos, even as the latter groups experience higher rates of unemployment.[23] They see opportunities for people like themselves contracting, while blacks and Latinos "feel there are a set of long-term opportunities that are opening to them that were previously closed on the basis of race or ethnicity."[24]

Data about racial disparities mask the experiences of working-class whites. Median wealth of whites is twenty times that of blacks and eighteen times that of Latinos, a gap that doubled as a result of the collapse of the housing market.[25] But working-class whites fall far below any median of white wealth. For many, the very idea of "wealth" being associated with their circumstances is laughable. The most recently reported median annual income for whites over age twenty-five without a college degree is $28,644, compared to $23,582 for blacks and $22,734 for Latinos who also only completed high school.[26] This reflects a greater than 20 percent income disparity, but the white person trying to live on such wages is much closer in circumstances to working-class blacks and Latinos than they are to whites higher up the income scale. When civil rights advocates discuss racial inequality or when progressive academics speak of "white privilege," what they are really comparing is the experiences of ordinary people of color to that of affluent whites.

Working-class whites are rarely disaggregated in these debates. They don't feel privileged, and they are not privileged in the globalized economy. Racial disparities in the poverty rate have narrowed significantly since 1970, and economic insecurity now threatens to engulf more than three-quarters of white adults by the time they turn sixty.[27] This may have something to do with why many whites shut down or become irritated by a classic civil rights discourse that almost always focuses on racial/ethnic disparities as a measure of inequality.[28]

Meanwhile, for many people of color, racial disparities are lived. If they are not seriously struggling, they are related to or know someone who is and often are called upon to give financial assistance to family.[29] Yet whites tend to blame blacks for their lack of advancement rather than structural barriers or inequalities.[30] Nearly half of blacks seem to agree with them, blaming themselves rather than discrimination for "why many black people can't get ahead these days."[31]

White folks in the age of Obama, in particular, are tired of hearing black complaints. His election seems to have exacerbated the perception gap about racial inequality. Even non-blacks who voted for Obama became less supportive of policies designed to reduce racial disparities after his election. A team of researchers discovered this ironic effect by surveying seventy-four undergraduates at the University of Washington immediately before and after the 2008 election. After Obama's election, "participants concluded that racism was less of a problem and that anyone can achieve success through effort and perseverance." Hence they expressed less support for policies like affirmative action, school desegregation, and other diversity policies.[32]

Levels of racial resentment toward blacks have also risen since Obama became president. In a 2012 Associated Press poll, 51 percent of respondents expressed explicit anti-black attitudes, compared to 48 percent in a similar 2008 poll. Those expressing such anti-black views were more likely to be Republicans (64 percent compared to 55 percent of Democrats).[33] The academics that conducted the poll did not measure anti-black attitudes as equivalent to racism.[34] An online comment to an article in the *New York Times* illuminates the difference:

> I'm a child of the rural South. But you know what? Actual racism is a lot
> less common there—we have a ways to go but there is real progress on
> that front. The more serious problem is white resentment. A lot of white

people honestly think they have been significantly deprived of various things because of minorities. And it's hard to overstate how deeply these feelings run. It's not so much animosity toward people who are different—it's the animosity of the aggrieved. They feel like they are victims.

Progressives are often perplexed at why blue-collar guys blame their economic frustrations on people of color and not Wall Street or corporate titans. This is a learned response. In the South, especially, ever since Reconstruction threatened to create a biracial democracy responsive to the working classes, economic elites have stoked racial tensions in order to avoid redistributive policies.[35]

Our black president is the latest, most convenient wedge issue.[36] Although working-class and poor people of all colors suffer greatly from this divisive politics, anti-government rhetoric has reached a frenzied screech in the Age of Obama. The angry black man has been replaced with the angry white one. Post-Obama, Latinos and blacks express optimism about their future chances while certain whites are deeply pessimistic and resentful. Old-fashioned racism has been supplanted by a much more subtle sentiment of racial resentment about not getting ahead. In the past, the primary emotion associated with negative racial attitudes was disgust accompanied by ideas about biological inferiority. Now anger is the primary emotional trigger for negative racial attitudes among whites who harbor them. Two political scientists find that "anger is uniquely powerful at boosting opposition to racially redistributive policies among white racial conservatives."[37] Nonracial ideologies and preferences for small government are not activated by these emotions.[38]

These negative racial sentiments in turn influence policy stances. Racial resentment often correlates with opposition to any policies perceived as redistributive. For example, another team of political scientists found that whites who registered above average in racial resentment were three times more likely than others to choose the least extensive version of health care reform presented to them in a survey.[39] Those who registered low levels of racial resentment were twice as likely to support a significant expansion of health care coverage.[40] They attribute this difference to differing gut-level worldviews. Partisan attachments, they argue, are increasingly shaped by visceral perspectives, such that even ostensibly nonracial issues are now also about race.[41] Not surprisingly, those who harbor racial resentments are more likely to support voter-identification laws and other provisions that make it more difficult to vote.[42] About thirty states have passed or are considering laws restricting access to voting, the vast majority of which have Republican governors or GOP-controlled legislatures.[43]

This is the latest iteration of the Republican Southern strategy, although changing demographics have rendered it a losing approach to presidential elections. With a GOP that has become utterly dependent on white votes, especially in racially gerrymandered districts, it is nearly impossible for some candidates and talk show hosts to resist the ease of tapping into a well of anger and resentment for votes and ratings. No candidate or commentator has to mention race. They need only stoke anger about government spending "your money," and voters who harbor racial resentments will make the connection in their minds, for "those people."

And so in the age of Obama, where "the primary negative emotion underpinning white attitudes towards blacks—anger—is so common in everyday life,"[44] even debates about infrastructure have become hyper-partisan. Race cleavages built into the architecture of our politics stymie progress on myriad fronts. For some whites, limited government values allow them to express race-based objections to redistributive policies without appearing racist.[45] This does not mean that all whites who oppose big government are racist or lacking in nonracial, small-government principles. Researchers are finding that where negative racial attitudes exist, they heighten partisan tendencies.[46]

Facts no longer matter in these debates. Emotions, culture, and worldviews do. According to other social science research, people tend to reject facts that do not fit with their cognitive frames of reference.[47] On matters of race, many if not most whites have a cognitive frame of reference that suggests to them that no interventions on behalf of racial minorities are necessary. The idea of prejudice is threatening to most whites' self-identity as nonracist. Thus they can protect their self-identity by minimizing perceived racism.[48] This may explain why blacks and whites can have dramatically different perceptions about whether a particular event, say George Zimmerman's profiling of Trayvon Martin, was motivated by racism. That perception gap was mirrored in reactions to the trial verdict: in a Pew poll, 86 percent of black Americans expressed "dissatisfaction" with the verdict, compared to only 30 percent of whites,[49] and in a Washington Post/ABC News poll, only 9 percent of blacks "approved" of the acquittal, compared to 51 percent of whites.[50]

Our politics of divided worldviews might be manageable if politicians had to compete for the votes of people with diverse visceral perspectives. But racial gerrymandering and our tendency to live among people like ourselves inhibit that possibility. The racial cleavage that typifies our national politics is most pronounced in the South. Political scientists who have carefully examined Southern politics conclude that race is the dominant issue. Blacks and whites appear to hew to a racial interest as opposed to an economic one. Large majorities of Southern blacks, regardless of income, identify themselves as core Democrats, while core Republicans outnumber core Democrats in every income category among Southern whites.[51]

There is a tight racial architecture to politics in the South that has been exacerbated by racial gerrymandering. Republicans dominate in districts that are 0–14 percent black; they are competitive in the districts that are 15–29 percent black; and they fail in districts with black populations above 30 percent. This pronounced racial structure dramatically shapes how and whether a politician can assemble a winning coalition. White Republicans espouse a robust conservatism designed to attract substantial white majorities, while black Democrats can be equally robust liberals.[52] The racial architecture of Southern politics does not leave any room for moderation, and it does not encourage cross-racial competition for votes or a discourse of racial empathy. Latino voters are beginning to complicate this dynamic. For them, unlike with non-Hispanic black and white voters, economic status roughly predicts partisan loyalties.[53]

Of course, the effects of racial gerrymandering are not limited to the South. Nationally, incumbents from both parties have excelled at propagating themselves such that only a few dozen congressional seats are competitive in each election cycle.[54] After the 2010 elections, however, Republicans in control of state legislatures elevated racial gerrymandering to a new level of precision, purging Democrats and people of color to create safe Republican districts that are much whiter than the country as a whole. As a result, the average Republican House district rose to 75 percent white—similar to America in the 1970s—while the white population in the average Democratic district declined to 51 percent—akin to what America will look like in the 2030s.[55]

Add to this racial gerrymandering the virtual gerrymandering caused by the echo chamber of social media, cable news, and talk radio, and polarization has reached toxic levels. A politician with 150,000 Twitter followers is the emperor of his parallel universe and feels no compunction about trying to impose his will on a national polity that doesn't agree with him. As the nation witnessed during the government shutdown and debt ceiling crises in the fall of 2013, incumbents running in safe, racially and ideologically homogeneous districts have no incentive to moderate.[56]

Beyond the effects of gerrymandering, the ideological and cultural sorting of America into separate places and separate states has greatly diminished the possibilities for robust democracy or for simply relating to the cultural "other."[57] As I write this chapter, one political party controls the governor's office and both chambers of the legislature in more than two-thirds of the states—the highest number in six decades. The GOP enjoys unified control in twenty-four states, nearly twice the number controlled by Democrats. Republicans control all of the legislatures in the states of the former Confederacy. Gerrymandered districts may have helped to elect large numbers of black state legislators in the South, but less than 5 percent of them serve in the majority party that dominates the region. And the GOP itself is hemmed in by the racial resentments of angry white voters that animate Tea Party activism and Republican primaries. With Congress held hostage by gerrymandered extremists, politics is broken in Washington, DC.

REFORMING AFFIRMATIVE ACTION
TO BEGIN RACIAL RECONCILIATION

Race-based affirmative action is but one of several touchstones in the code-worded discourse that helped create this divided state of affairs. Our nation lives with political gridlock borne of racial cleavage. The ascendance of political conservatism in the late twentieth century—an ideology of limited government, individual responsibility, and traditional values—coincided with the ascent of an ideology of color-blindness, and the one fueled the other. As Harvard professor Jennifer Hochschild has argued, opponents of affirmative action gained cultural and political traction in part because their message fit with our most cherished values: the promised dream that in America anyone can prosper, regardless of race, sex, or other background, through sheer ambition and hard work.[58] This ideology of individualism, in turn, animates the anti-government attitudes of Tea Party purists and consequent Republican obstructionism in Congress.

In light of this backlash, those who continue to champion race-based affirmative action must consider whether its benefits are worth the costs of continued racial divide. Empirical studies of the impact of affirmative action show that the policy did help to create the black middle class. But, according to Hochschild's summary of the empirical literature, affirmative action was not nearly as influential as other, less controversial strategies like antidiscrimination enforcement, raising educational achievement of students of color, and reducing barriers to voting and holding office. While affirmative action had critical influence in raising minority presence at selective colleges in the 1980s, at the non-elite schools that 80 percent of college students attended, it seemed to play little to no role in admissions.[59]

The relevant debate is not whether we should have had affirmative action in the first place. That question is moot. Given the inevitable demise of race-based affirmative action, the relevant question is, what is its logical replacement? Political constraints borne of a perception gap between whites and non-whites about the need for government interventions to redress racial inequality are likely to harden with rising demographic diversity. Institutions necessarily are changing to accommodate both emerging racial complexity and globalization. Latino enrollment in US colleges grew by a whopping 24 percent between 2009 and 2010, an increase of 349,000 students. In the same one-year period, enrollment by blacks and Asians also grew, while non-Hispanic white enrollment fell by 320,000.[60]

This new America is threatening to many whites. Ironically, if you define merit solely in terms of test scores and grade point averages, many whites will fail in head-to-head competition with global aspirants for whom the Ivy League are safety schools. World strivers from Mali to Malaysia who don't mind spending six, eight, or more hours a day studying compete with American applicants and, in the eyes of admissions officers, may even be viewed as more deserving.

Some increases in diversity will result naturally from demographic change. With the browning of America and the pressures of globalization, all institutions face a diversity imperative in order to maintain relevance and market share. White anxiety will continue to rise as more and more whites experience a loss of majority status. D. A. King, a Georgia activist against immigration reform, recently said explicitly what many whites may feel: "I was taught that we have an American culture to which immigrants will assimilate," he said. "And I am incredibly resentful that's not what's happening anymore."[61] Between the lines, he seems to be equating "American" culture with whiteness, and this dislocation of his tribe as the dominant political and cultural force in the United States is what most rankles.

In less than three decades, majority-white America is going to be replaced by multi-racial, multi-ethnic America. This transition is already creating social conflict—a conflict of values, culture, and political philosophy. Some voters, including many white ones, embrace diversity as a positive value and want the communities they live in, the employers they work for, and the governments they vote for to reflect their own openness and tolerance. They are averse to policies that ostracize particular groups, be they LGBT people, undocumented immigrants, or racial minorities. On the other hand, in a flat world where globalization and technological change are causing a great deal of economic pain, growing racial complexity threatens others. The philosophy of a small, color-blind government that takes no cognizance of racial and ethnic difference and touts "traditional" values resonates with voters who feel dislocated or disoriented by America's racial and economic transitions.[62]

These emotions and negative attitudes are not going away, and can't be willed away. Voters tend to believe what they have been told, and if a political party builds a politics based upon racial loyalty over decades, it can take just as long to undo the damage. Gunnar Myrdal's articulation of our American dilemma continues, but racial resentment supplants racial prejudice as the cause of our failure to realize our ideals. As two researchers who identified the potency of anger in current politics put it: "We think solving the problem Myrdal laid out over seven decades ago remains a challenge in contemporary America because it will involve breaking the powerful linkage between anger and ideas about race."[63] If whites are to engage with diversity rather than resent it, the rules of competition must be perceived as fair to them and everyone else.

CHAPTER TWO

Place Matters

In 1964 my parents enrolled me in an all-black nursery school, Fellowship Presbyterian. The school and church were not far from the campus of Alabama A&M University—a bastion of black educators and a source of social uplift and protestors in Huntsville's successful sit-in movement. (Nonviolent demonstrators like my mother, who was arrested with me as an infant in her arms, convinced the Rocket City to desegregate its public accommodations in 1962.) At Fellowship my teacher, Mrs. Gardner, would greet me with hugs and kisses. She was family, part of an intimate black world that prayed and played together. My parents loved their people, but they were also integrators. My father always said that politically he was a Baptist but intellectually he was a Unitarian. He had found camaraderie with the scientists and free-thinkers that populated Huntsville's Unitarian church. Even better, in that community he had found white activists to participate in the sit-in movement and irritate what he called "the white power structure." Our family joined the Universalists and religiously attended services that were more hippy-humanist than spiritual.

By age five I had developed some of my parents' cultural dexterity. Mrs. Gardner thought I needed more stimulation than Fellowship could provide, and I did not mind it when I became the only black child at Grace-Lutheran, one of the few private schools in the city that would accept a Negro kindergartener.

I continued as an integration pioneer when I entered first grade at Blossomwood Elementary, an all-white school. A few years earlier, a boy named Sonnie Hereford IV had overcome George Wallace's obstructions to become the first child to integrate a public school in the state of Alabama. Sonnie's parents and mine had been lead conspirators in Huntsville's movement. Once they earned the right to order a hamburger at a Walgreens, they had turned to the schools. My two older brothers and I would be the first to color Blossomwood, although Dad had to use a ruse to get us into that attendance zone.

Blossomwood had the only program in the city for hearing-impaired children, and my parents were determined to get one of my brothers into it, but no one in the neighborhood would sell to a Negro, much less an uppity one. After two years of trying and failing to buy a house in this all-white neighborhood, they conspired again with the Unitarians to undermine a race code. My parents had become especially close to two families in the church. Activism had blended into friendship and weekends in which the parents hosted unruly parties and the children spied on them from below. One of these families bought a house for us in the Blossomwood District with Dad's money. Our new next-door neighbor immediately sold his home to a Jewish buyer.

When integration was new, this is what it meant—a few, willing pioneers entering previously all-white spaces, sometimes aided by a lawsuit and federal troops, sometimes because of bloodless audacity. Most of the integration America achieved still fits that paradigm. Families of color with the wherewithal to buy their way into gold standard neighborhoods are welcome. Meanwhile, the demarcation between favored quarters and everywhere else has become sharper.

Place matters. In 1954, Linda Brown's brown skin was what kept her out of the school of her choice. Sumner Elementary was blocks from her house, in an ethnically diverse neighborhood in Topeka, Kansas. The school board forced the third grader to walk across railroad tracks and then take a bus to get to Monroe Elementary, a segregated school for Negro children. Linda Brown's father, Oliver, became the lead plaintiff in *Brown v. Board of Education*. Today, a family of color does not need to file a lawsuit to attend their neighborhood school, although about two-thirds of black and brown kids are being locked out of high-quality schools because of where they live.

In the geographic sorting that goes on in metropolitan areas, everybody aspires to live in a neighborhood that helps them to get ahead. The children of parents who can't afford to escape to quality are stuck in segregated, high-poverty schools. This is the modern meaning of *Brown v. Board of Education.* Those who can afford to integrate will, assuming the cost is worth it to them. Those who can't are relegated to less opportunity or, in some ghetto neighborhoods, no opportunity. Our nation did not pursue a transformative integration in which institutions and neighborhoods were redesigned to make opportunity broadly available to everyone. Place, although highly racialized, now better captures who is disadvantaged than skin color.

Brown did pay real dividends to students and society in the era when the Supreme Court and the federal government enforced it vigorously.[1] Research shows that children of all races and incomes who attend integrated schools improve their critical thinking skills, are less apt to accept stereotypes as truth, lead more integrated lives as adults, and are more civically engaged. Racial minorities in integrated schools also achieve at higher levels, with no detriment to the learning of white students.[2] A primary benefit of *Brown* today is psychic. Within one generation from that edict, America transformed from a country in which most people accepted white supremacy and racial exclusion as the natural order to one in which most people did not.

When the Supreme Court declared in *Brown* that separate could never be equal, it was following through on the Party of Lincoln's promise of equal protection, made in 1868 with the adoption of the Fourteenth Amendment. The Radical Republicans first introduced this idea of equality into the Constitution to ensure that African Americans would be full citizens. Equality was a revolutionary concept that required destruction of race hierarchy. The most radical Republicans imagined a new society in which all could participate on equal terms. For a fleeting moment, Reconstruction threatened to do that. The city of New Orleans integrated its schools in 1870, and the black and white students who learned together outperformed their segregated counterparts.[3] But it was too much, too soon. Interracial cooperation was an affront to economic elites who prospered when workers were pitted against each other. Race lines were redrawn by white supremacy Democrats and maintained by law and terror throughout the South.

Not much had changed by 1954. The *Brown* Court renewed the promise of full citizenship to African Americans that it had ignominiously denied them in *Dred Scott*.[4] No child could be expected to succeed in life, Chief Justice Warren wrote, without the opportunity of an education, and any state that undertook to provide an education had to make it available on equal, unsegregated terms.[5] That, too, was a militant concept. If the Court's vision of a universal, free, equal education were to be realized, it would require a transformation of the entire system of education, what law professor colleagues refer to as "radical integration."[6] Instead, courts pursued desegregation rather than transformative inclusion, placing the burden of assimilation on integration pioneers. *Brown* bars states and school districts from purposely erecting racial barriers to integrators of any color. Because of limitations imposed by the Supreme Court, its work stops there.[7] No one can be excluded based upon skin color. But no one can be included based solely upon race either. In 2007, the Court barred school districts from pursuing integration in a manner that takes the race of individual students into consideration.[8] If a community wants to create transformative integration in which all groups share in the benefits and burdens of diverse schooling, it must do so creatively, without using racial preferences and without much assistance or encouragement from the federal government. And it must buck a trend of geographic separation of the affluent and the poor.

THE ROLE OF PLACE

In theory, America is an integrated land, one where a black man can be elected president twice. In practice, separation of the races and classes is common. The average non-Hispanic white person in metropolitan America resides in a neighborhood that is 75 percent white.[9] The typical African American lives in a neighborhood that is only 35 percent white. In the largest metro areas, most black people live in neighborhoods where they predominate. Latinos are less segregated than black folks, but they also tend to live with *la gente* and have very few white neighbors. Asians are the most integrated of so-called minorities. On average, the largest share of their neighbors is white. Thus whites, blacks, Latinos, and Asians tend to experience diversity very differently in their daily lives.[10]

This differential experience of place greatly affects opportunity. Only about 30 percent of black and Latino families reside in neighborhoods where less than half of the people are poor.[11] Put differently, less than one-third of black and Latino children get to live in middle-class neighborhoods where middle-class norms predominate. Meanwhile, more than 60 percent of white and Asian families live in environs where most of their neighbors are not poor. As urban sociologist John Logan put it, "It is especially true for African Americans and Hispanics that their neighborhoods are often served by the worst-performing schools, suffer the highest crime rates, and have the least valuable housing stock in the metropolis."[12]

Race appears to play a more dominant role than class in determining where one lives. Even affluent blacks and Latinos suffer from neighborhood inequality. In the last two decades, black and Latino families with annual incomes above $75,000 were more exposed to poverty, on average, than poor whites making less than $40,000.[13]

The good news is that racial segregation is less pronounced than it used to be.[14] In 1950, about half of black people lived in ghettoes. Now only one in six black folks live "in the 'hood."[15] In 1950, eight of ten black people would have had to move in order to be thoroughly integrated in America. In 2010, about six out of ten black people would have to move, assuming integration mattered to them.[16]

Asians and Latinos are much less segregated than African Americans, although their levels of segregation have not changed in thirty years, in part because these groups are growing so rapidly.[17] Asian and Latino populations grew at nearly forty times the rate of growth of the white population between 2000 and 2010. This helps explain why it is now difficult to find what we used to refer to in the South as a "lily white" neighborhood. There are very few census tracts in metropolitan America that are 100 percent white.[18]

While housing segregation declines modestly for blacks and whites, economic segregation has been increasing. The number of neighborhoods with intense poverty and the number of people living in them has risen dramatically since 1970.[19] Most of the families living in ghetto neighborhoods have been stuck there for generations.[20] Race and class segregation persist in part because of discrimination in housing markets, weak antidiscrimination enforcement, and snob zoning in which affluent towns intentionally prevent affordable housing, even apartments, from invading their turf.[21] The Fourteenth Amendment prohibits state and local governments from promoting racial exclusion, and most jurisdictions would disavow such intent. That the state is not intentionally promoting apartheid seems irrelevant to children who endure isolation. Whether intended or not, racial and economic segregation beget inequality, which in turn affects the debate about whether and how to maintain affirmative action.

Five decades of social science research demonstrate what common sense tells us. Neighborhoods with high poverty, limited employment, underperforming schools, distressed housing, and violent crime depress life outcomes. They create a closed loop of systemic disadvantage such that failure is common and success aberrational. Even the most motivated child may not be able to overcome unsafe streets, family dysfunction, a lack of mentors and networks that lead to jobs and internships, or the general miasma of depression that can pervade high-poverty places. Professor john powell—an expert on equity and inclusion who intentionally spells his name in lower case—likens living in a high-poverty context to running up the "down" escalator. One study by the Pew Center found that a high-poverty 'hood virtually guarantees downward mobility.[22] Living in a severely disadvantaged neighborhood impedes the development of verbal cognitive ability in children, correlates to a loss of a year of learning for black students, and lowers high school graduation rates by as much as 20 percent.[23]

At the other extreme, those privileged to live in high-opportunity neighborhoods rise easily on the benefits of exceptional schools and social networks. As powell surmises, it is like riding on the "up" escalator. Anyone who has spent time in high-opportunity quarters knows intuitively what this means—the habits you observe, the people and ideas you are exposed to, the books you are motivated to read. Social mobility is still possible for those blessed to live in job-rich, low-poverty environs. And this geographic structure of opportunity is highly racialized. The majority of whites and Asians live in neighborhoods with a poverty rate below 14 percent, while large majorities of blacks and Latinos do not.[24]

These are not statistics that whites want to hear about. It may trigger what social scientists call "cognitive shutdown," such is their fear of being labeled a racist if they enter any debate about race or their weary perception that they are being blamed for societal ills they did not cause.[25] But this isn't a blame game. In fact, the same forces that create geographic disadvantage for many blacks and Latinos also disadvantage average white folk.

In an American metropolis stratified into areas of low, medium, and high opportunity, place is a disadvantage for anyone who cannot afford to buy a home in a premium neighborhood.[26] The iconic, picket-fence spaces that once nurtured middle-American dreams have shrunk along with real wages. A recent study found that only 42 percent of American families now live in middle-class neighborhoods, down from 65 percent in 1970. This is due to the rising segregation of the affluent and the poor from everyone else. While income segregation has grown fastest among black and Hispanic families, high-income families of all races are now much less likely to have middle- or low-income neighbors.[27]

In the past, escaping poverty and its real or imagined consequences meant a move to the suburbs. But the geography of poverty is expanding. More poor people now live in suburbs than cities, and concentrated poverty is growing fastest in the suburbs.[28] This change can be found in older, majority-white suburbs, where the Great Recession and winnowing out of middle-class jobs have hit hard—places like Lakewood, Ohio, a streetcar suburb of Cleveland built in the early 1920s to provide homes for factory workers at local plants that have shuttered. At Lakewood High, less than 10 percent of students received free or reduced lunches in the prosperous 1990s. A decade later, nearly half were poor.[29]

The same story has been repeated in suburban hamlets across the nation. With the deindustrialization of the US economy, a local factory or steel mill that provided union-wage jobs closes, and a white suburban ghetto of sorts emerges as a result. Middle-class habits like marriage have eroded with the economy. The jobs that are available don't pay much. The tax base of such towns shrank with the exodus of large employers, and the semi-skilled workers who remain struggle to pay rising property taxes. Immigrants willing to do low-wage work and those attracted to the cheaper housing stock find their way to these towns, placing more demand on schools, some of which are literally crumbling. Three-quarters of homes foreclosed on during the crisis were in suburbia.[30] And struggling suburbs with more than their fair share of affordable housing, eroding infrastructure, a weak tax base, and an influx of immigrants and urban movers are not receiving much help or guidance on how to be diverse successfully.

Most white people living in struggling suburbia are stuck in place too. Only those who can acquire the high-level skills and educational credentials that global employers require have the possibility of moving to the relatively small number of cities and college towns where the highest-paying jobs are clustered.[31] Since 2000, a lot more native-born, high school, and even college-educated whites live in thickets of suburban poverty.[32]

Bonnie and Andy, a middle-aged, formerly middle-class couple, lost jobs and their home to foreclosure, one of many new homeless families in the Jefferson County suburbs west of Denver. They and other families rent weekly at a budget hotel off I-70 in a strip of cheapness that ski tourists bypass. Bonnie drives her son to his middle school in Bear Valley, a neighborhood of well-kept ranch homes, hoping their new circumstances will not be discovered. She and her family spend all of their free time in Bear Valley, going there to shop, buying less, eating daily at the hot-food bar at their favorite grocery store. She drives back and forth, straddling her old world and her new, shabbier one, trying to hold on to a semblance of her past life. She feels angry and helpless, reserving most of her fury for Countrywide Financial, the company that issued a usurious subprime mortgage to her family and caused them to lose a home that had been paid for.[33]

Another suburban mom enjoys a different lifestyle. Gayle Patton and her family live in a planned community called Fall Creek in Humble, Texas. She and her husband decided to move to this suburb 15 miles from downtown Houston for a larger home and better schools. Segregation was not their purpose but when they looked at what the market offered and where their friends were, they were drawn inexorably to this wooded enclave with its own golf course and elementary school, spacious yards, vaulted homes and neighbors in the same economic bracket. Most of the homes in Fall Creek require an income or assets that would place residents in the upper ten percent of earners. "I think every other house out here has a lawyer in it," she told a *Houston Chronicle* reporter. "I'm not kidding." Both Gayle and Dan Patton are lawyers, and this community has worked well for their family of five. Patton has Asian, Latino, and African American neighbors, but no blue-collar ones.[34]

What happens in a society in which income and wealth are increasingly concentrated in certain neighborhoods? Two researchers that documented these trends reasoned that bastions of affluence create disadvantage elsewhere.[35] Sociologist Douglas Massey also invokes Charles Tilley's phraseology and calls it "opportunity hoarding." Massey argues that where social boundaries conform to geographic ones, the processes of social stratification that come naturally to human beings become much more efficient and effective. In his words: "If out-group members are spatially segregated from in-group members, then the latter are put in a good position to use their social power to create institutions and practices that channel resources away from the places where out-group members live." The same power can be used to "direct resources systemically toward in-group areas."[36] In plain English, place locks in advantages and disadvantages that are reinforced over time. Geographic separation of the classes puts affluent, high-opportunity communities in direct competition with lower-opportunity places for finite public and private resources. And affluent jurisdictions are winning, sometimes because they are subsidized by everyone else.[37]

Rising geographic separation of the affluent, then, appears to contribute to rising inequality.[38] A nationwide study by economists at Harvard and Berkeley found that upward mobility for poor children varied greatly depending on where they lived. The East and West Coasts do better than the heartlands. Seattle, Salt Lake City, and Boston afforded much greater possibility for a poor child to rise up the economic ladder than Atlanta, Charlotte, and many cities in the South and Midwest. Researchers did not pinpoint exact causes, but segregation of the poor from middle-class people was a strong correlating factor. Places that had a sizeable middle class and enabled poor families to live among them had higher rates of mobility.[39]

This study is consistent with research showing that America has much more of a class system than other developed nations. Contrary to our favored shibboleths, it is much more likely in America than in other advanced economies that a child's life chances depend on the class of her parents.[40] What is becoming more evident is the role of place in under-mining social mobility. Income inequality has risen dramatically since 1970, at the same time that "masters of the universe" were becoming ever more residentially isolated from the average Joe or Jamila.[41] The ratio of CEO-to-worker pay has increased 875 percent since 1978.[42] For megamil-lionaires and billionaires who live in enclaves of exclusion, it may be easier to make class distinctions because they are not familiar with folks who struggle. It may be easier to justify allocating larger shares of corporate revenues to those at the very top of the income scale and to the owners of capital, rather than to wages of ordinary workers. Segregation has cer-tainly made it easier for the financial industry to prey upon certain neigh-borhoods and borrowers.[43]

Segregation of the highly educated has increased even faster than that of the affluent. Only seventeen counties in America have a popu-lation in which more than half are college educated.[44] Marin County north of San Francisco; Orange County in North Carolina's research triangle; Boulder County, Colorado; affluent suburbs bordering Wash-ington, DC; and New York City are in this club. In the vast majority of US counties, college graduates are a small minority.[45] College graduates used to be more evenly distributed, but segregation between them and high school graduates has nearly tripled since 1940.[46] Highly educated people are drawn to metro centers where other people like themselves live, and within the metropolis they gravitate to neighborhoods of their own kind. This phenomenon transcends race. College graduates living in America's most highly educated metro areas are more residentially iso-lated than African Americans.[47]

This concentration of human capital in some places and not others has consequences for children. Some kids, like mine, grow up in environs chock-full of doctors, lawyers, World Bank economists, prize-winning journalists—the list goes on, and the networks are deep. This intellectual density greatly raises expectations and provides a steady flow of shared wisdom about what it takes to get into a great college. As educational elites congregate in their own universes, the standards and networks for entry into the leadership class become more foreign and less obtainable to those who live elsewhere. A dean of a prestigious law school said of the trend: "Those that are afforded a high-quality selective K-12 public education enter elite colleges and become leaders, and everybody else gets to watch on television."[48]

PLACE AND CHILDREN

Children are more segregated than adults, and public school children are more segregated today than at any time in the last thirty years. School segregation has risen rapidly since the Supreme Court indicated in the 1990s that it was time for federal courts to stop policing school desegregation orders. As school districts across the country reverted to neighborhood schools, racial segregation surged, especially in the South. The overwhelming majority of Latino and black students (80 and 74 percent, respectively) now attend majority non-white schools. Meanwhile, the typical white student attends a school that is 77 percent white.[49]

Exposure to poverty at school is also typical for black and Latino children, and much less common for white and Asian kids. The average black or Latino public school student attends a school where nearly two thirds of her peers are poor, almost double the share of poor kids that the average white or Asian student experiences.[50] A recent study of the hundred largest metro areas found that 43 percent of black and Latino students attended schools where more than 80 percent of the kids were poor. Only 4 percent of white children went to a school defined by poverty.[51]

What most endures about *Brown v. Board of Education* is its seminal finding that separate is inherently unequal. Racially segregated, high-poverty schools often have "less experienced and less qualified teachers, high levels of teacher turnover, less successful peer groups and inadequate facilities and learning materials," all of which limit educational outcomes.[52] I once asked a friend who worked as a mental health counselor in Baltimore City Schools what could be done to counter the poverty that overwhelms some schools, and her fatigued answer was, "Just pray." Given that most black and Latino kids suffer the disadvantages of segregation, no one should be surprised that they lag whites and Asians in math and reading on standardized tests.[53] Sociologist James Coleman first reported in 1966 that the primary predictor of school performance is the socioeconomic background of the children. Coleman concluded that the social composition of the student body was more highly related to a child's achievement than any other factor, including per-pupil expenditure, class size, and teacher experience. This groundbreaking insight has been confirmed by decades of subsequent research.[54]

This does not mean that poor kids are stupid. But policies that concentrate poverty are. Different policy choices produce better outcomes. Montgomery County, Maryland, a diverse suburb adjacent to Washington, DC, has chosen inclusion over separation for four decades.[55] When it enabled black and Latino residents of public housing to move to a middle-class neighborhood and attend middle-class schools, the children did much better than those they left behind. The county also put extra resources into its high-poverty schools. This enabled a researcher to compare the math and reading scores of children of public housing. The movers were much more successful than the children given extra resources.[56] This, too, accords with prevailing social science. Middle-class schools perform much better, for poor children and everyone else.[57]

The Obama administration has placed its hopes not on tackling the forces that concentrate poverty in schools but on trying to turn high-poverty schools around. That strategy has failed.[58] To be fair, so has every federal program of the last half-century that tried to overcome concentrated poverty with additional resources.[59] *Only one percent of high-poverty schools succeed.* Those rare outliers that do produce enviable outcomes benefit from conditions that are not replicable for all high-poverty schools.[60] Geoffrey Canada's much-touted Harlem Children's Zone, which provides "cradle to college" supports for children and family success in a one-hundred-block area, spends $90 million annually. While they are lifting children up, the Zone's charter schools have produced mixed results.[61] The KIPP network of charter schools—consistently top performers—succeed in part by attrition. Only the most motivated of families apply, and only the most motivated of students stay.[62] The rest are left behind in the 99 percent of high-poverty schools that do not succeed.

By 2020, the majority of all children in America will be non-white.[63] Segregating many of them into high-poverty schools is a poor strategy for promoting America's future. Countries with high-performing education systems place their most talented teachers in disadvantaged schools and channel more resources into those schools, the opposite of what we do in the United States.[64] Higher poverty in American schools usually means less experienced or burned-out teachers, fewer resources to meet greater needs, and an oppositional culture that tends to denigrate learning.[65]

I call it the undertow. A child surrounded by poverty is not exposed to other kids with big dreams and a realistic understanding of how working hard in school now will translate into concrete success years later. This oppositional culture has been identified not just in high-poverty African American and Latino communities but also in high-poverty white areas. Researchers debate its existence.[66] Ask any black achiever who attended public school about it, and many will recall a question that dogged them: "Why you acting white?"[67]

In my tribe of African American, hypereducated parents, the stories and fears of the undertow abound. There's the brainy black son who left public school for a Jesuit institution where it felt safe to be a geek. He listened to hip-hop on the Metro, then reverted to the Frank Sinatra he loved when he was beyond earshot of disapproving race police in his teenage cohort. There are the black achievers at Wilson, the best-performing neighborhood public high school in Washington, DC. According to hearsay, they survive and thrive only by keeping invisible in advanced tracks that separate them from the general population. One Wilson alum told me about a fellow black classmate who lived in the upper-middle-class "Gold Coast" of DC, drove his mother's Mercedes, and brought a gun to school, such was the pressure he succumbed to "to be ghetto." Such performance art and the lore it generates influence the choices of parents who have alternatives.

The swagger of "thug life" arose from the ghetto, like Tupac's rose from concrete, a code of survival in a dystopian world.[68] It has become a venerable stereotype of blackness, one that has sunk deeply into the subconscious of most people of all races.[69] And this pervasive stereotype has a lot to do with why it is so difficult to correct policy mistakes like segregation and mass incarceration. We can't realize the ideals of *Brown* because we are too afraid of the code of the street. Meanwhile, the children trapped in high-poverty environs pay the highest price for our moral failures.

The challenge of overcoming negative cultural influences in high poverty settings is one of the reasons I have steadfastly advocated for race and class integration, even as that goal sometimes feels quixotic. An alternative to school integration would be to dramatically reduce class size and place excellent, experienced teachers in the most impoverished schools.[70] This, too, feels like an irrationally idealistic strategy in a time of partisan gridlock and public scarcity.

Separate but unequal schooling presents parents with stark choices. My husband and I were blessed to find each other and procreate late in life. We are middle-aged parents to twin six-year-olds in the center of an educational arms race. In Washington, DC, we observe the choices of other professional parents of color; precious few send their child to a segregated, majority-black public school. Most of them bypass that experience. Some literally win the lottery for a scarce out-of-boundary spot at a school in an affluent neighborhood or at a high-performing charter school. The rest send their kids to private school or move to a whiter and wealthier neighborhood west of Rock Creek Park, or to Bethesda or some other suburban quarter that guarantees quality, at least for now.

All of us are affirmative action babies. We attended good schools or got a job because we worked harder than the competition, but also because an affirmative action policy forced an institution to cast a wider net. None of us are betting on affirmative action to get our kids into Harvard (although some wince at the idea that legacy preferences may be eradicated just as a sizeable cohort of colored folks is ready to use them). Instead we are doing the same things that other high-income parents around us do. Hiring tutors, signing up for Kumon drills, language-immersion classes, summer math camps—whatever it takes to gain a competitive advantage or just keep up. We are no different than other parents in our aspirations for our children. All of us will avoid a high-poverty school, but our choice is largely dependent on whether we have the means to do so.

There are some schools and neighborhoods that buck the dominant trend of racial and economic segregation. Sometimes it happens organically. Usually it requires intention. A neighborhood association decides to fight blockbusters who exploited white owners' fears and Negro buyers' desires for better housing. That is the history of Shepherd Park, just east of Rock Creek Park, in Washington, DC, where my family lives. After the Supreme Court rendered racially restrictive covenants unenforceable in 1948, blacks and Jews could buy homes in this neighborhood of large lots and mature trees that developers had advertised as "high class" two decades before. Many whites and Jews did leave after the riots of 1968, creating an enclave of African American professionals and white liberals who were comfortable living among them. Since the 1960s Shepherd Park has remained an integrated neighborhood, a fitting tribute to its namesake. (Boss Shepherd, the post-bellum governor of the District, was infamous for profligate spending and self-dealing on public works; lately he has been rehabilitated as a Radical Republican who modernized the federal city, integrated its public schools, and advocated for emancipation and black suffrage.)

Shepherd Elementary School is not as integrated as the neighborhood that surrounds it. The school is 79 percent black. Nearly a third of its students are on free and reduced lunch. Only 28 percent live in the neighborhood. To its credit, Shepherd offers a rigorous International Baccalaureate curriculum and greater opportunity to kids whose parents could not afford Shepherd Park. And the school is doing nearly as good with black students in reading and math as sought-after west-of-the-park schools.

My family is one of the many in our neighborhood who chose private school over Shepherd Elementary. It started in a guilt-free way. When our boys were two years old, private school was the only option. We chose Aidan Montessori, the same wonderful school that my husband had attended as a toddler. Then, three years in a row, we tried and failed to win the lottery to get our sons into exceptional public charter or west-of-the-park schools. Each year we took a close look at Shepherd and noticed marked differences from other schools on our wish list. The number of kids on free and reduced lunch kept rising at Shepherd. On tours of the school we noticed things in need of repair—a broken water fountain, a toilet that didn't flush, loose door hinges and a physical plant that looked like it had not been updated for several decades. (As I write this chapter, much-deserved renovations have finally begun at Shepherd.) Inside the classrooms, children were learning, but it gave us pause to see a clutch of eager children commanding a teacher's attention at the front of one room and a smaller cadre of restless kids at the back not being engaged by anyone. This pattern was repeated in another classroom. There was much to offer a focused kid, but our cumulative impression was one of risk.

We were shocked by the abundance of riches at Janney Elementary. Like all the other highest-performing schools in the district, Janney is located west of the Park, not far from American University. Janney's $29 million renovation and expansion includes a soaring atrium and a modern science lab, while Shepherd and other schools have none. My husband was particularly impressed by Janney's new library, which was outfitted with a computer lab holding a bank of Apple computers and an open reading area with plush pillows lit by floor-to-ceiling windows. Janney has an art studio with a pottery kiln, high-tech white boards and projectors in every class room, a beautiful playground, and gardens the students work in as part of their science studies. The school also happens to be adjacent to a new, architecturally stunning public library with row upon row of books to capture a young person's imagination.

Janney also has a very different school population than Shepherd. Only 7 percent of its children are black and only 2 percent are poor. Over 90 percent of Janney students are from the surrounding neighborhood. Precious few out-of-boundary kids enjoy this magnificent public school. On the school tour, an electric sense of engagement wound through every student. My husband and I were impressed and considered moving to the Janney district. But after several months of visiting open houses, we decided against paying the nearly seven figures for a smaller house and yard and few or no black neighbors.

We eliminated other west-of-the-Park neighborhoods for the same reason. I had experienced being the only black girl for miles as a young child and I wanted something different for my children. In Shepherd Park our sons could walk out the front door and see professional black families in every direction. They also would live among non-blacks who willingly moved to a neighborhood where they were a minority. These families understand diversity because they live it. Hopefully they will continue to smile at rather than fear our boys as they get older. We felt confident that a Shepherd neighbor would not mistake them for a stranger and call the police in an unexplained situation. Living here, maybe our children would not think about race on most days. I manage the magical thinking of color-blindness only in small communities of trust—fellow writers and activists, beleaguered parents of rambunctious children desperate for a play date, a neighbor who loves my children and brings them gifts on every holiday. Staying put, with a manageable mortgage that made it easier to pay for private school, felt like the wisest option.

Our private Aidan Montessori school offered a superior education and racial diversity, although there were no poor kids in the school. It had four teachers from four different races or ethnicities among its primary classes. And it had three or more African American boys in each of those classes. We had listened to stories of African American parents at other independent schools who had endured years in which their son was the only black boy in a class. We didn't have to lobby or educate administrators at Aidan about the value of diversity. Nor did we have to deal with insensitivities that had driven some parents to withdraw from another independent school. Aidan worked, but it felt obscene. By our fourth year we were paying $24,000 per child, plus thousands more spent on caregivers, summer camps, swimming, music, tae kwon do, Spanish and Mandarin lessons. We continued to explore other options.

Other families we knew were sacrificing even more. An African American parent who sends his children to the same exclusive private school that Sasha and Malia Obama attend told me that he was spending $75,000 annually for two young children, such were the pressures to donate to the school even after making full tuition payments. In 2013 this was the price of the ticket in Washington, DC, for first-tier independent schools that pave a secure path to selective colleges.

A wife of an Obama Cabinet member seemed ambivalent about the choices her family felt compelled to make. "These schools take very talented children and make them feel below average," she told me. She confided that in this stratosphere parents often spend another $10,000 a year on private tutors. Another African American mother who has her daughters in premier independent schools was more pointed: "These schools will f*ck your daughter up," she said over drinks. "I have to constantly deal with their esteem issues." She was speaking of how a black girl in a school with few of them doesn't get asked to the dance, doesn't feel beautiful or valued. A black male at a posh school can have a cultural currency that non-black kids might want to tap into. White girls might want to date him. White guys might gain cool points by being his friend. "If I had to do it over again, I would do something different," this frustrated mom said. "What?" I asked. "I don't know, move!" She didn't have an answer for where her utopia might be. So her daughters stay in hyper-elite schools because she can afford it and the educational rigor they offer renders this the best among limited options.

My family won the public school lottery on our fourth try. Our odds were enhanced because another parent at an open house happened to mention that our dream school ordered its wait list based on the date one applied. Who knew? The online applications for the Washington Yu Ying Public Charter School opened at 8:30 a.m. on a Tuesday in October, and we hit the send button at 8:31. In April, Yu Ying sent us an e-mail inviting one of our sons to enroll in first grade. The other son was next on the waitlist. My elation was tinged with guilt. There were scores of other families below us on the waitlist. Each year, thousands of children are disappointed by the DC school system lottery as they vie for a chance to attend a better school than the one in their neighborhood. Across America, millions more families are also waiting for the equal education they deserve.

RADICAL INTEGRATION IN SOME PLACES

At Yu Ying, families willingly travel across geographic and cultural boundaries for a Mandarin-immersion international baccalaureate program that money cannot buy, at least not in the District. Any family residing in the city can apply and entrance is awarded solely by lottery. No high-stakes tests or interviews are required. The school is located in Northeast Washington in a majority-black zip code near Catholic University. Its dynamic principal is African American. In 2012, the student population was 48 percent black, 27 percent white, 18 percent Asian/Pacific Islander, and 7 percent Latino. One-fifth of the children were low-income and 9 percent had special education needs.

The day my husband and I visited for a new parent orientation, the kids appeared to be one happy rainbow. It seemed a much friendlier place than a few of the snark-laden comments on DCUrbanmoms.com suggested. The school's academic intensity and 100 percent Mandarin immersion in the early grades is not for everyone. Our tour stopped in a pre-K classroom, and I watched something I had never seen.

Four-year-old miniature people were separated into two teams, all urgently raising their hands, fighting for the opportunity to go up to the blackboard and write the answer to a math problem: $5+3 = \_\_$. My kids had been introduced to math concepts early at Aidan Montessori, but they did not begin to abstract, to do math facts at age four. My jaw dropped. Two gorgeous, aubergine colored boys jumped up, racing to see who could write "8" first. A diminutive Chinese woman taught this math class in Mandarin. She played the lead in this musical, the cadences of her happy shouts washing over the kids' heads. They shouted back in Mandarin—order, learning, fun. Stunned visiting parents marveled at the excellence their tax dollars could produce and worried about whether their own kids would measure up to Yu Ying's exacting standards.

Several parents testified online that they had left private schools for Yu-Ying. One said that she could not believe such a wonderful school was free. They had come to immerse their child in an ancient language and culture that is not European. To enter diversity without fear, decoupled from where one lives, to obtain language and social skills that are rewarded in the global marketplace, Yu Ying offered the kind of radical integration that the *Brown* decision hinted at. Most charter schools in the United States are racially and economically segregated and do not outperform traditional schools.[1] The strong demand for Mandarin immersion seems to have spared Yu Ying that fate. It helps that Yu Ying occupies a beautiful, renovated 1902 building on a three-acre lot that offers playgrounds, a sports field, and an outdoor natural learning area. It is a public school that has drawn people with options back to the public square. And they are sharing their resources with less fortunate kids rather than hoarding them in neighborhoods and schools of their own. Members of the Yu-Ying board donated $50,000 to send fifth graders on a three-week trip to China—a reward for being the guinea pigs in the first class of this brave new adventure.

Above all, for my family and others, this imperfect school is very good. It is making impressive gains every year for advantaged and disadvantaged students learning in two languages.[72] It shows that radical integration can attract more families and resources to public schools by being free, diverse, and good enough.

The magnet school movement has produced many more inspiring institutions that transcend stark neighborhood boundaries. Magnet schools were created in part as a response to the negatives of "forced busing." When school systems listen to parents and build the unique, world-class programs they want, they will come. More than one-third of black and Latino children in Hartford, Connecticut, now attend racially and economically integrated schools, although the vast majority of them live in low-opportunity neighborhoods.[73] This school integration is radical compared to what existed before thirty-one interdistrict magnet schools were created and over twenty suburban school districts welcomed Hartford children into their classrooms.

As with *Brown*, sometimes it takes creative lawyers to bring about a transformation. A fourth grader named Milo Sheff and other kids trapped in racially isolated schools sued the state of Connecticut in 1989, and seven years later the Connecticut Supreme Court issued a ruling that rankled many adults and politicians. The court found that Milo and all other children in the state had a constitutional right to an equal education, and that the state had to take affirmative steps to overcome local government boundaries that were the key cause of racial isolation. Opponents fought the ruling in the legislature. Eventually the adults negotiated solutions to the problem of boundaries. They built magnet schools in Hartford and surrounding suburbs. Suburban school districts agreed to open up places at existing schools for Hartford children. A new multiracial coalition of parents that like and advocate for integration and school quality rose up. They call themselves the Sheff Movement.

They are not alone. Four scores of school districts in America currently use economic integration strategies that give parents choices and a shot at quality. The other 14,000 do not.[74] Districts that have not given up on integration have read Justice Kennedy's words carefully. They take this aging man at the center of the Court's ideological spectrum at his word. Even as he voted to strike down Seattle and Louisville's race-conscious school integration plans, he said in the *Parents Involved* case that school districts are not required to accept "the status quo of racial isolation in schools." He endorsed their right to experiment, to "seek to reach *Brown's* objective of equal educational opportunity."[75] With school integration plans, as with affirmative action, Kennedy is sympathetic to the project of creating diversity, so long as individuals are not excluded because of their race. And so the outlier districts keep trying, sometimes because of a lawsuit, sometimes because people of good will organized and came together for the common good.

In the metropolis, there are many residents who like and are drawn to diversity. They delight in difference and mash-ups of people in public spaces where no one group dominates. Their rising comfort increases possibilities for remaking schools and neighborhoods that mirror this multicultural ethos. Like Richard and Mildred Loving in 1967, whose interracial marriage produced the Supreme Court's breakthrough decision in *Loving v. Virginia*, these optimists cross racial lines daily for love, friendship, or just to have dinner. For me, now, this is what integration means.

Integration is real inclusion, what I see when my family goes to Downtown Silver Spring on a summer evening. At this outdoor mall, a beautiful fountain inlaid with a primary colored mosaic resembles the many-hued, screaming children who splash in its waters. Every race, ethnicity, and class seems to be represented here, perhaps with the exception of the extremely affluent. This privately owned fountain is the ultimate public good. Everyone is welcome to enjoy it. Entrance is free. There is no exclusion or exclusivity in this space, and everyone seems to revel in the sheer diversity of humanity drawn to it. The people here are culturally dexterous. By "cultural dexterity" I mean the ability to enter a space where you are outnumbered by people of a different race or ethnicity and feel comfortable, not threatened. If you have had a meal in the home of someone of a different race recently, you are probably culturally dexterous.

In integrated milieus all groups, including formally dominant ones, assume some responsibility for creating a society in which public and private institutions, schools and neighborhoods mirror the robust and accelerating diversity of our nation. In an optimistic, inclusive America there would be no ghettos. No school or neighborhood would be overwhelmed by poverty. Black and brown children would be valued and included as much as any other children because the fear associated with high-poverty 'hoods has ebbed as they have become mixed-income places where middle-class norms prevail.[76]

When it comes to education, unfortunately, federal and state leaders focus mainly on reducing racial achievement gaps for children stuck in segregated schools. And yet there is no consistent evidence that the No Child Left Behind (NCLB) law has been effective nationally in narrowing achievement gaps. In fact, there is some evidence that NCLB may have widened achievement gaps.[77] Given these modest effects and the

drudgery heaped on millions of children being taught to pass standardized tests, it is unfortunate that accountability has replaced desegregation as the touchstone of education reform. There are new and better
strategies than busing. Magnet schools, inter-district choice programs,
high-quality inclusive charters like Yu Ying, and other fresh ideas can
work for all kids.[78]

If we deconcentrated poverty, we wouldn't struggle so much to "reform" racially identifiable schools. We wouldn't have so many dropout
factories. We would have fewer problems that government and society
must respond to. Integration makes it easier, not harder for middle-class
families and parents to raise high-achieving kids. But divisive politics
that paint government as the enemy make it difficult to make shrewd
investments in programs that work. Until more people organize for the
common good, tired scripts will continue to play out. A neighborhood
or school reaches a tipping point, becomes identified as a black or brown,
those with options flee, and systems only work for the most affluent.
Meanwhile, race-based affirmative action does little to help segregated
youth overcome the systemic disadvantages they face because other, more
economically advantaged people of color can trade on their skin to benefit
from racial preferences. Most selective colleges are passing over the strivers at low- and medium-opportunity schools in favor of the most culturally palatable of colored people, those with a track record of achieving and
assimilating in elite settings.

CHAPTER THREE

Optical Diversity vs. Real Inclusion

Each year millions of young people apply to college or some other post-secondary program. Half of them focus on nonselective four-year schools or two-year community colleges that are not difficult to get into, but shockingly few students graduate from. These nonselective institutions confer degrees on only about half to a third of entrants because they have far less resources and faculty to support students than those allocated to selective higher education.[1] The other half of the national applicant pool aims higher, setting their sights on colleges with competitive admissions. Affluent students aim highest. Like their parents, they believe that selectivity is their ticket to self-sufficiency in a post-industrial global economy that has shed millions of middle-class jobs. Each year, the number of applicants trying to enter our nation's most elite schools climbs, and the percentage accepted declines. Spaces at the top are finite. Aspirations and anxiety are without limit. Harvard received over 35,000 applicants for the class of 2017 and accepted only 5.8 percent, to create a class that will be nearly half non-white.

The Great Recession accelerated the flight of the affluent to perceived safety. As with K-12 education, those with resources seek the highest quality they can obtain. In part because of skyrocketing costs, the pool of applicants to highly selective schools has become whiter and wealthier as the pool for nonselective institutions has become browner and poorer.[2] Yet globalization and demographic change prod all institutions to diversify. The *US News & World Report* rankings also propel colleges to chase after students with the highest test scores in an escalating bid for selectivity.[3] The debate over affirmative action is about who gets into selective schools, and those segregated into lower-opportunity environs are almost invisible in this argument. Economic elites of all colors enjoy built-in advantages in the withering competition for spaces at choice schools, and the children of Hagar blessed to inhabit elite campuses are usually on familiar turf.[4]

A young man who attended Dartmouth in the mid-2000s recently described his experience to me. I will call him Trey. The son of a white mother and a black father, Trey graduated from a large urban public high school where a kid adroit at negotiating honors tracks and all-black social contexts could thrive. He self-identifies as both black and white, not an amalgam of the two. Like Obama, he can code-switch between "standard" English and beloved cadences of one strain of American blackness. "I was shocked at how few students there were at Dartmouth who came from backgrounds I could relate to," he told me. According to Trey, most of the people of color on campus had already learned the ways of the masters of the universe while attending Groton, Hotchkiss, Deerfield, or well-regarded high schools located in bastions of suburban privilege. "It took me a while to figure out how things worked," he said. "The person I had the most in common with was a white guy from a small town. The students of color were not that different from the white students in terms of what they had been exposed to."

When he arrived, Trey's class was touted as the most diverse in Dartmouth's history, a refrain repeated about subsequent entering classes. (According to recent reports, 36.4 percent of Dartmouth undergraduates are non-white or multiracial and 16 percent receive Pell Grants, federal financial aid for low-income students.) "They had diversity in appearance but not necessarily in experience," Trey said of his time there. Now he is in law school. We spoke via Skype while he was on a lunch break from a public interest internship. He said this of his years at Dartmouth:

> I was middle class. My mom worked for city government [as a lawyer]. My father sorted mail at the post office. I was used to going to school throughout my life with a very broad spectrum of incomes and living

situations. I went to public school my whole life. At Dartmouth, I felt like a fish out of water. My roommate couldn't understand why anyone would ever sell drugs. He went to Exeter. I told him, "You are caught up on this as illegal. It's just economics. If you live somewhere without any possibilities and you can make hundreds of dollars in a night, you are going to do it." Not many people understood why people in poverty did things they did or why they didn't do what others thought they should do. There was this perception that the poor got what they deserved. Not many people understood structural obstacles. That would undermine their own success. . . . The black people on campus thought I was ghetto because I spoke a certain way. There were major pressures from both sides. No one was going to make me choose between being mainstream or being black.

Trey was speaking of the Faustian choice between hanging with the "black community" on campus with its own rules of racial solidarity, or joining in the predominant culture propagated by majority-white frat houses. When I asked Trey why he related best to a small-town white guy, he answered:

Because he went to public school. His father was a carpenter and a part-time store clerk and his mom was a homemaker. He became a teacher. Like me, he just wanted to go to a good school and explore what it had to offer. He didn't go to Dartmouth for its name. He was more able to see people as individuals without caring what frat they were in or what their dad did. I could teach him [black urban] slang and he would use it appropriately, without being judgmental. We were both free to be ourselves and pursue our own interests. Not the kid who made it out and had the weight of carrying their whole family out with them. And not crushed by a family legacy, where you're expected to go to a T14 school, get your MBA, head to Wall Street, join the country club, send your kids to the same schools you went to, and continue the cycle.

Trey discovered Dartmouth on a visit to see his white grandparents, who lived nearby. "I got no letter from Dartmouth, although Harvard wrote to me," he said. His high school counselor discouraged him, told him he would not get into either school, even though he had a 3.8 GPA and took six AP classes. (He passed five of six AP exams.) He was in a strong magnet program within his high school, placed there because his middle school counselor had believed in him and encouraged him to apply for the competitive program. Three other black males from his middle school who entered the magnet program with him succumbed to the undertow, pulled back into easier general classes. Trey explained it this way: "None of your black friends were taking hard classes or talking about the SAT and AP exams. So it becomes a question of why am I busting my butt with these white kids when my boys from the basketball team or neighborhood are clowning in an easier class and getting just as good grades?"

Trey's contrarian ways helped him. He is comfortable with himself and exudes quiet determination that is obvious in a face-to-face interview but wouldn't be translated by a standardized test score. He got into Dartmouth in part because he paid close attention to the habits of his peers in the magnet program. "I picked up on what they were doing and I was motivated to show them that I could compete." His magnet peers also provided the most useful information he received about how to prepare for and apply to competitive colleges.[5]

Although he is middle class, Trey's story is of a piece with recent research about low-income strivers. A 2011 study about disadvantaged black male achievers accepted at highly selective colleges found that few attended regular schools in their neighborhood. Most had gone to magnet schools with a challenging specialty curriculum, a college-preparatory culture, and a competitive admissions process. Others had the good fortune to participate in a program like Prep for Prep that took them out of their resource-deprived urban school, put them on campuses like Phillips Academy Andover, and continued to nurture and counsel them through the college admissions process. The Posse Foundation also changes lives for those who emerge from a rigorous selection process, giving them a scholarship, mentoring, and a crew of other urban strivers to attend the same college with. New zero-loan initiatives created by well-endowed universities have also helped to raise the number of low-income black male achievers at highly competitive universities.

The stories uncovered by this study are heartwarming. One participant, Kareem, had a 3.3 GPA and an extensive record of leadership in high school. His guidance counselor repeatedly told him to apply to community college. "To me, [that] would have been a failure after I had worked so hard," he told an interviewer.

"I told her I wanted to apply to better schools and asked, 'How can you help me?' She persisted and insisted that I apply to community colleges. It got to the point where I had to rip the application up and threw it at her. 'I'm not going to apply.' After that we didn't have any more talks about college. It wasn't until I got the Posse scholarship that she tried calling me in to show me off to other parents. But yet two weeks prior, she couldn't help me out with finding any colleges."[6]

Kareem attended DePauw University. I am happy for him, and for Jerrell, another Posse scholar who spent most of his childhood in the Vanderveer housing projects in Brooklyn but also made it to the expensive private school in rural Indiana that Vernon Jordan attended because of the good works of the Posse Foundation. Their example and Posse's is laudable. The problem with programs like Posse and Prep for Prep is that they can save precious few kids from the deprivations of weak schools and neighborhoods. Others will be left to their own devices in trying to overcome myriad structures of disadvantage, and statistics suggest that few of them are succeeding. Only 7 percent of young people from the bottom quartile of socioeconomic strata graduate from college.

The exemplars interviewed in this study said they knew other black males from their neighborhoods who would have followed their path of success if they had been given access to the same opportunities for preparation and financial support.[7] There are many kids with grit trapped in circumstances beyond their control. What they need most is not affirmative action but fair systems of opportunity and a college admissions process that does not exclude them.

In fact, the pool of disadvantaged strivers is much larger than many would imagine. Economists Caroline Hoxby and Christopher Avery have garnered headlines for their research about low-income high achievers. They estimate that the number of low-income high school seniors who break the 90th percentile on the SAT or ACT and have a GPA of A- or better ranges from 25,000 to 35,000 each year.[8] Nearly 6 percent of this cohort is black. Nearly 8 percent is Latino. In other words, each year between 3,300 and 4,600 high-achieving, low-income black and brown youth graduate each year. This number does not include middle- and upper-class black and Latino achievers. About 200 poor Native American youth also meet this standard every year. Over 17,000 poor white achievers and 3,800 poor Asian achievers fill out the cohort.

Three or four thousand low-income black or Latino high achievers may seem paltry. Let me put these numbers in perspective. The above-mentioned study of low-income black male achievers focused on a sample from eighteen highly selective predominantly white private schools, including Amherst, DePauw, Harvard, Stanford, and Wabash College. In 2008, a total of 300 black males of *all* socioeconomic backgrounds attended sampled institutions. Black male presence on these admired campuses ranged from a low of 1.4 percent at Saint John's University in Minnesota to a high of 5 percent at Stanford. Proponents of affirmative action might argue that these numbers underscore why universities must consider race in admissions. But low-income high achievers of all colors are poorly represented at selective schools, in large part because of geography, not race.

THE ROLE OF PLACE IN ADMISSIONS

Selective schools begin excluding achievers in lower-opportunity places through their recruitment process. It starts with standardized tests. Schools use them as a search tool (in addition to over-relying on them as indicators of "merit"). They can buy mailing lists of high-scoring students from the College Board, which administers the SAT, and from ACT, Inc. Highly selective schools tend to prefer the SAT over the ACT. If they buy mailing lists only from the College Board, they will miss all high-scoring students that take only the ACT. The ACT is favored by students in the South and middle of the country, while the SAT is favored on the East and West coasts. Catharine B. Hill, president of Vassar, and Gordon Winston of Williams College estimate that selective schools miss more than six thousand very high scoring, low-income students each year simply because of their SAT-only search policies. A school with an SAT-only lens would miss more than half of the highest-ability students in Alabama and Michigan.[9]

Geographic bias continues with outreach. Obviously a college cannot send admissions officers to visit all 42,000 high schools in America. Choices must be made, and selective institutions tend to visit high schools that are reliable feeders or are located where plenty of high achievers from other schools can also get to a presentation. If a college recruiter wants to reach a critical mass of high achievers in one trip, the most efficient and well-travelled route is to areas dense with college-educated parents: urban counties in southern New England, the Mid-Atlantic region, southern Florida, or coastal California or large cities like Chicago, Houston, Dallas, or Atlanta.

Hill and Winston suggest that such traditional recruitment patterns explain why selective private schools fall short in their representation of low-income, high-ability students. They focus on parts of the country with small numbers of low-income achievers and neglect regions with a lot more of them. Midwest and mountain states produce 21.2 percent of low-income high achievers nationwide, while New England is home to only 3.5 percent of them.[10]

Place influences not just where colleges choose to recruit but also where achievers choose to apply. Hoxby and Avery set out to understand why thousands of low-income high achievers do not apply to selective schools that would cost less because they can offer more financial aid. Low-income achievers who lived in neighborhoods with higher numbers of college graduates tended to behave like higher-income achievers. They applied to safety schools, schools with median test scores that mirrored their own, and to some stretch schools, and they persisted to graduation after enrolling, as those with "college knowledge" typically do. Hoxby and Avery labeled these students "achievement typical" because their approach to college was typical of non-poor achievers. More than 70 percent of achievement-typical students came from just fifteen large urban areas, each of which is home to one or several selective colleges. These places included the usual suspects: San Francisco, Oakland, Los Angeles, Dallas, Houston, Chicago, Boston, New York, and Philadelphia. Most of the low-income achievement-typical students came from a small number of high schools—magnet or independent schools that admit students on a competitive basis.[11]

Hoxby and Avery concluded that many selective colleges were "searching under the lamppost."[12] They look for low-income students where the college is located rather than where these students can be found in large numbers. The low-income achievers under the streetlamp are already more likely to apply to and attend selective colleges. Admissions officers spend much time reaching out to the lamppost high schools that have already been cherry-picked by their competitors, contributing to the perception that the pool of disadvantaged achievers is miniscule while doing little to increase the college-attending behavior of strivers who live elsewhere.[13] One anecdote illuminates the narrow lens of elite admissions offices. The Yale College Class of 2009 was drawn from roughly 900 high schools, even though economists at Harvard conclude that there are more than 10,500 schools that offer students of sufficient caliber to enter Harvard (and, presumably, Yale).[14]

Hoxby and Avery found that low-income achievers not privileged to live in neighborhoods thick with college graduates or to attend a school where college knowledge is pervasive behaved differently. They applied to fewer schools, and the vast majority did not apply to selective schools. Hoxby and Avery labeled them "income typical." On average, only 3.8 percent of an income-typical student's peers were also high achieving, compared to 11.2 percent for achievement-typical students. Income-typical students also tended to live in neighborhoods where few people attended a selective college. Given where they lived and went to school, their probability of meeting a teacher, counselor, schoolmate, or friend who attended a selective school was negligible.

Peers also matter. A student who does not have rich parents that can pay a private consultant to help them negotiate the admissions process desperately needs good advice and information. Every high school in America has a valedictorian, but low-income ones tend to be in lower-opportunity schools, where they receive worse guidance than their lower-performing classmates because high school counselors tend to focus on colleges and practices that fit the general population. Recent valedictorians from public high schools report that their school counselors were "lousy," "incompetent," or "woefully lacking."[15] Without good guidance, low-income achievers tend to pursue colleges that are already familiar to them and the people around them, reinforcing the influence of place and class.

Low-income achievers, in particular, need information tailored to help them overcome their worries about debt. Hoxby and economist Sarah Turner discovered that a well-designed brochure that cost only $6 per student to produce and mail induced income-typical achievers to apply to selective, better-resourced schools.[16] If a selective school is sincere about achieving socioeconomic diversity, then it must recruit differently to find the many poor achievers that do exist.

Hoxby and Avery's income-typical achievers were much more geographically dispersed than achievement-typical students. About 80 percent of them were white.[17] Place disadvantages poor whites differently than it does low-income students of color, who are more likely to grow up in high-poverty neighborhoods. It would be counterproductive to engage in an "Oppression Olympics," comparing the obstacles of growing up poor, rural, and white to the challenges of overcoming concentrated poverty. The truth is that low-income students of all colors—even high-achieving ones, even valedictorians—are being overlooked by selective campuses because of geography. Place creates disadvantages that are different in kind than racial discrimination. Place is not a proxy for race. Race is a social construct, place is a physical one. They are distinct phenomena that need to be understood on their own terms. In college admissions, perhaps unintentionally, place often operates to exclude. Meanwhile, admissions officers who think about race are not typically using it, as in the past, as a basis for exclusion. For an underrepresented minority, race can be a plus factor that enhances that person's chances of being accepted.

WHO COUNTS AS BLACK?

The same forces shaping diversity in the work place put pressure on colleges and universities to reflect the rainbow on campus. A veteran director of admissions at a select university labeled this "institutional vanity." I will call him Jonah. We spoke in his office on a quiet Friday morning in September. He had just welcomed the new entering class he had helped shape and was proud that he had managed to attract many students of color without sacrificing the school's all-important standing among peer schools. "We all worry about the complexion of the class," Jonah said. "Among the schools in the top 20 or 30 in [*US News & World Report*] rankings, we all consider race."

Jonah explained to me the brutal practicalities of creating diversity on elite campuses. "It is much more true than not that as schools are looking to fill the 'black' or 'Latino' column, they don't care about the socioeconomic background of the kid or where the kid comes from. Wealthy kids . . . Obama's kids, wherever they come from, each one counts as one," he said. Jonah was speaking not of quotas but the optics of the classroom. Professors, administrators, and many students want to look across a room and see a human rainbow. The son of an African World Bank executive or the daughter of a black president counts the same in terms of optics and is easier to admit than the son or daughter of a black policeman.

The challenge is especially difficult with African Americans. As Jonah explained, the common wisdom among admissions officers at the highest-ranked schools is that the pool of black talent that can compete "by the numbers" without consideration of race is very small. (Although, as I argue above, geographic bias in recruiting skews these perceptions.) The higher-ranked an institution, the higher its median SAT scores for its entering class, the more relevant affirmative action becomes.[18] In these elevated halls of achievement, race-based affirmative action can produce unintended consequences.

One of the perverse aspects of the optical diversity currently being pursued at very selective colleges and universities is that it redounds to the benefit of children of African immigrants, who, on average, are the best educated of all immigrant groups. Among the undergraduates that might be counted as black at Harvard in 2012 were fifty-seven students from Africa and the Caribbean. Nigeria and Ghana were the highest feeder countries. According to an analysis of census data by the *Journal of Blacks in Higher Education*, Africans who have come to America are better educated than *any* native-born ethnic group, including whites and Asians.[19] Almost half of all African immigrants in the United States are college graduates, a rate slightly higher than that of Asian immigrants, nearly twice the rate for native-born whites and nearly four times the rate of college attainment for native-born blacks.

In recent years an average of about 62,000 Africans have been immigrating to America annually, more than the numbers that were brought forcibly each year during the height of the slave trade.[20] They and their West Indian counterparts are complicating the meaning of blackness in America. About 30,000 blacks immigrate from the Caribbean annually, and this region contributes the largest share of black immigrants at selective colleges (43 percent), followed by Africa (29 percent) and Latin America (7 percent).[21] Today one in three blacks in New York City are foreign-born. In head-to-head competition at selective colleges, many black immigrants can trade on their skin more easily than African American slave descendants because they tend to have better academic credentials.[22] And, if speculation of researchers is to be believed, they are less threatening or more palatable to white admissions officers than "homegrown" black people.

Connie Jackson, a Harvard-educated African American business consultant who lives in London, speculated about the Africans' competitive advantages in the eyes of non-blacks: "They just get it done. They are untouched by racism. They bring a very strong work ethic. They don't complain. They have an accent, which helps. It makes them exotic." Connie was not "hating" her African cousins; she suggests that American blacks emulate them. "We need to be more diasporic, if that is a word. Like the [native and repatriated peoples of India], we need to build alliances.... In global markets it's hard to talk about minority unfairness, because there are so many unfairnesses."

Some of the cultural advantages experienced by Africans who come to America may stem from the fact that they tend to settle in more integrated settings than native blacks. According to a study of students of color at twenty-eight selective undergraduate institutions, because native blacks tend to live in blacker neighborhoods than do immigrant blacks, they experience more violence and disorder as they come of age. Native blacks were also less likely to attend private schools than immigrant blacks. Nearly three-fourths of native blacks attended public high schools, compared to only 58 percent of black immigrants.[23]

Because they tended to live a more integrated existence, black immigrants were more likely to have non-black friends. They also appeared to be significantly less susceptible to peer influences than black natives, apparently because those who maintained an immigrant identity were better able to insulate themselves psychologically from other youth they encountered at school or in the street.[24] This advantage of place for immigrants shows up in other studies. As two researchers who examined the question concluded: "Whites, Asians and recently arrived, foreign-born blacks generally live in the best quality neighborhoods, and Hispanics and native-born blacks have the worst neighborhood conditions."[25]

The most critical difference between native and immigrant blacks at elite schools, however, seems to be in educational attainment of their parents. The fathers of black immigrants are far more likely than those of native blacks to have obtained undergraduate and advanced degrees.[26] These relative advantages of black immigrants translate into success in university admissions. According to a study published in the *Sociology of Education*, selective colleges enroll only 2.4 percent of native black high school graduates but 9.2 percent of black immigrants (and 7.3 percent of all whites).[27]

Ironically for proponents of affirmative action, black American descendants of slavery might fare better under programs based upon segregation or structural disadvantage rather than race.[28] A disadvantage-based diversity program might better approximate the actual obstacles that many native black children face on the path to college. For those native blacks who are not disadvantaged, Connie Jackson said to me of the state of global competition: "There is someone who is reading by candlelight in Ghana. They may walk five miles each day to get clean water. They are working fiendishly, trying to get to where they have the luxury of doing nothing but study. And when and if they do, they will clean our clocks."

While black immigrants, on average, live in better neighborhoods and have more education than native blacks, this does not mean that they are immune to racial discrimination or hardship. The modern African diaspora is as complicated as the human spectrum. A black immigrant from a multiracial society that experienced racism prior to moving to the United States faces more difficulty than other black immigrants in getting ahead.[29]

Lani Guinier, a Harvard law professor, and Henry Louis Gates, former chairman of Harvard's African and African American studies department, began an uncomfortable conversation a decade ago about why only about a third of black students at Harvard were from families that descend from slaves. The debate quickly turned to whether "the descendants" who were the initial intended beneficiaries of affirmative action should remain so.[30]

A recent acquaintance, a Ghanaian American, argues that she and others like her need and deserve affirmative action. "Jane" was born in Harlem Hospital to Ghanaian immigrant parents. Her mother had entered a difficult marriage to a Ghanaian American that brought her to America and earned her citizenship. After divorcing, Jane's mother parked her five children with her own mother in a housing project in the Bronx. She worked two jobs as janitor and hotel maid and studied nursing, eventually earning a degree and more income. Later she married another Ghanaian immigrant who fits the profile of patrimonial educational advantage that I described above. Jane's new stepfather had been the cleverest boy in his village, picked from among thousands for a scholarship to study in the United States. He became a neurologist—only in America, at least for dreamers of a certain age.

Jane was raised by her grandmother and lived in the projects until age twelve or thirteen. Her mother lived thirty minutes away in a modest rooming house near her two jobs. The arrangement enabled Jane's mother to avoid the time and cost of daily commutes. It was typical of Ghanaian immigrant families. A breadwinner goes wherever a livelihood can be made, pays the bills for the family, and an elder raises the young. Jane's mother was intent on getting her children out of the projects. She sent them to parochial schools, saved every spare dime, and managed to buy a home in a middle-class suburb in Pennsylvania. Jane recalls being extracted from the projects just about the time she was developing physically. The timing was critical to her current success, she thinks. Jane was the oldest of her four sisters and she believes her emerging curves added urgency to her mother's exit strategy. She remembers that young girls in her housing project were constantly sexualized. They walked a gauntlet of catcalls every day. Usually their initiation to sex would come too soon and not on their terms. Many girls were pregnant by age sixteen.

In the suburbs, Jane continued to live with her grandmother and siblings. Her mother and stepfather remained in the city to work. The suburbs provided a better environment, but it was not idyllic. They encountered threats from the KKK. Other immigrant families were finding their way to this white middle-class outpost, and not everyone was happy about the transition. Jane remembers being surrounded by other immigrants. Buses would take African and Jamaican parents off to work in the city at 5 a.m. She attended a very good public middle school but recalls that school boundaries were redrawn to channel all the dark kids into the same school, and school quality eroded. For high school, Jane's mother put her back in a Catholic parochial school. It had a strong college preparatory program and Jane was the only black person in her grade. She didn't need affirmative action to get into the University of Pittsburgh, which she attended as an undergraduate. Her grades and SAT scores were on par with Pitt's medians. Jane is convinced she benefited from affirmative action when she entered graduate school at the University of Michigan on a full scholarship the year before Michigan voters banned the practice. She had this to say about it:

> I did benefit, and I should have benefited. My mother was very much a part of the narrative of black poverty in America. She came here with nothing and had to make tremendous sacrifices to get her children educated. A lot of what I experienced in the projects is also part of that narrative. My mother really did identify with what it meant to be black and female . . . the challenges and the discrimination. For a while she was a single mother on the WIC program. She needed my grandmother to help with childcare. She was very committed to policies that promote the interests of black people in this country. The real racism we experienced started when we moved to Pennsylvania. We inherited the distrust of white people that is more typical of black Americans than Ghanaians. Most Ghanaians in Africa worship the British. I always felt like the black struggle in the US was my struggle.
>
> I believe that I am deserving of affirmative action but I do think that there are people who are more deserving than I am. One of the biggest reasons I was able to go to college and finish was because I was able to move out of the projects. The [youth I left behind] are more deserving.

Jane thinks her mother, who came to America poor and uneducated, is more indicative of the typical African immigrant than her ultimately highly educated stepfather. "I know more people who are here illegally than legally," she told me, who have limited class mobility as a result. "They drive a cab, save some money, and go back to Ghana and start a business." Perhaps the demographers and researchers who report relative educational advantages for African and black immigrants compared to native ones are presenting a picture mainly of legal immigrants. I told Jane that I thought her mother typified the stereotype of the striving immigrant. I also conjectured that perhaps she was able to move her family out of a ghetto neighborhood because she had not lived in one before. Her poverty was not multigenerational, American-style ghetto poverty. She possessed resilience, resourcefulness, and the unbroken spirit of the African collective, the same collective self-help that propelled her stepfather out of his village and across the Atlantic.[31]

I think it is wonderful that families like Jane's enrich the meaning of American blackness. I view them as reenergizing the African American values of striving that undergirded W. E. B. Du Bois's Talented Tenth. That said, when an elite school uses race-based affirmative action to create optical blackness but little socioeconomic diversity, it masks the struggles of those who are limited by the places they have been relegated to. It may even make it easier to blame those trapped by segregation for their failure to overcome. Certainly, it puts no pressure on institutions or society to dismantle a system in which only those who escape to higher-opportunity environs prosper. Again, as I wrote in chapter 2, only one-third of black and Latino children get to live in middle-class neighborhoods. As one black admissions official at a highly selective college told a *New York Times* reporter:

> If somebody does not start paying attention to those who are not able to make it in, they're going to start drifting farther and farther behind . . . You've got to say that the long-term [native] blacks were either dealt a crooked hand, or something is innately wrong with them. And I simply won't accept that there is something wrong with them.[32]

Neither will I. There was nothing wrong with Trey or Kareem or Jarell or the children in housing projects in Montgomery County who were allowed to move and attend better schools. They all achieved when given meaningful opportunity.

The achievers in low-opportunity places that rise, despite the undertow, deserve special consideration from selective schools. They have enormous fortitude and focus—skills they had to develop to succeed against ridiculous odds, skills that will help them persevere through college. And it should not matter what color they are or what nation they come from. I agree that Jane was deserving of affirmative action, not because she is black but because she rose above tough circumstances. As I argue in the next chapter, colleges should reform their admissions processes in a way that enables them to discern these critical noncognitive skills and count them as merit. It is one thing to earn an SAT score of 1200 from a posture of privilege, it is quite another to do that from a difficult setting. As with Trey, anyone who took the time to interview Jane would immediately sense the inner-strengths that propel her. Both of them, a mixed-race African American and a first-generation African immigrant, would be captured by a holistic admissions process that took into consideration the structural disadvantages they had to overcome. Neither of them deserve special consideration simply because they can check the "black" box.

I recognize that what I am writing is sacrilegious in the civil rights community. "People are going to think you have lost your mind," my sister-in-law told me. We are both mothers of African American boys who could benefit from race-based affirmative action, although we are trying to raise lions that don't need it. "Our children will be okay," I told her. Other people's children, who are being crushed under the weight of unfair structural disadvantages like segregation, will not—not if we don't try to change the systems set against them.

"MERIT AID," EARLY ADMISSIONS, AND THE PERNICIOUS INFLUENCE OF *US NEWS & WORLD REPORT*

US News & World Report doesn't publish a magazine in print anymore. It makes money by ranking schools, cars, hospitals—causing institutions to scurry to conform to its weighted formulas. When it began ranking American colleges and universities, it injected an element of absolute competition between selective schools. They began to weight standardized test scores and grade point averages more heavily because that is what *US News* valued. As a result of this direct competition, many schools also adopted new strategies designed to attract or "buy" students with the highest GPAs and test scores.[33]

One tactic was early admissions. Early decision/action usually bene fits the wealthier, better-informed, and well-connected applicants in the pool. Students at less competitive public schools are not typically among this group. Yet early admission students account for 20–75 percent of those who matriculate to elite colleges. Racial minorities, public school students, and financial aid applicants are much more likely to apply in the regular pool, with its reduced odds of admission.[34]

Another tactic that arose in response to the *US News* rankings was to abandon need-blind admissions and increase a practice known by the euphemism "merit aid."[35] Language matters, and "merit aid" elides exclusion. I will use the term, grudgingly, because that is what everyone calls it, although it reminds me of the military's use of "collateral damage" to describe dead civilians. In the Ice Age, when I applied to college, "financial aid" was reserved for people with financial need. "Merit scholarships" were awarded to a relatively few exemplars, regardless of income. Now public and private colleges grant merit aid to higher percentages of their students than those who receive need-based aid.

The US Department of Education's most recent analysis of the trend is revealing. In 1995–96, 43 percent of students at private, nonprofit colleges and universities received need-based grants. Back then, only 24 percent received merit aid. By 2007–08, only 42 percent of students received need-based aid while 44 percent received merit aid.[36] Admissions directors at moderately selective schools engage in this practice more aggressively than those at schools comfortably ensconced in the top tier. More than half of students at moderately selective schools now receive merit aid, compared to only a third in the 1990s.[37]

The practice hits the poorest students and racial minorities hardest. As I will describe in depth later, the primary determinant of an SAT score is the socioeconomic background of the applicant's parents. Imagine a student who doesn't have much money but did well enough to enter a selective college. Unless she scored very high on a standardized test—not likely, because she is not affluent—she won't qualify for "merit" aid. Unless the school is very rich, she is not likely to receive a no-loan aid package. Other students who qualify for aid but do not suffer the disadvantages of low income or segregation likely will be eligible for merit aid. Sophisticated students and their parents have grown adept at playing the game and asking for it. As with the applications process, students who go to high school in more advantaged settings are more likely to understand how the financial aid system works and play the game accordingly.

Research shows a direct trade-off between awarding merit scholarships and enrolling lower-income students. One study found that as the share of institutionally funded National Merit Scholars increases in a school's freshman class, the share of Pell Grant recipients in its student body declines.[38] Another found that the introduction of a merit aid program led to a reduction in both black students and low-income students, particularly at top-tier schools.[39] Hill and Winston examined trends at fourteen very elite schools between 2001 and 2009 and found that most of the growth in financial aid given out by these colleges was allocated to the wealthiest of eligible students.[40]

This story gets worse. The US Department of Education requires colleges and universities to calculate and report their average "net price" for students that receive financial aid, as opposed to the "sticker price" that those who do not qualify for aid must pay. Anyone with Internet access can find out the net price of their dream school on the Department's College Navigator website. A recent analysis of this data found that hundreds of public and private colleges expect the poorest students to pay annual tuition bills that equal or exceed their families' yearly earnings. The cost is highest at private, nonprofit colleges. Only a few dozen exclusive colleges are able to meet the full financial need of the low-income students they enroll. Nearly two-thirds of private institutions charge students from the lowest-income families—those making less than $30,000 annually—a net price of over $15,000. Public universities charge less, but the problem is growing worse. As states cut funding for higher education, public colleges have begun the same kind of enrollment strategies pursued by private institutions.[41]

Several states have contributed to this trend of allocating financial aid based on merit rather than need. Twenty-five states have adopted merit scholarship programs in which lottery or tax revenues are used to give awards to achievers to attend home state institutions.[42] Most of these programs operate in the Southeast, which has the highest proportion of merit aid recipients (24 percent compared to 10 percent nationwide).[43] Professors Rubenstein and Scafidi at the University of Georgia found that Georgia's HOPE scholarships widened the gap in college attendance between students from low-and high-income families and that the scholarships were most likely to be awarded to students from high-income counties.[44] Another analysis found that HOPE scholarships increased car sales in the state, presumably because parents absolved of paying college tuition could buy them for their children.[45]

The states that award merit scholarships spend much less on grants based on financial need.[46] The consensus among researchers who have looked closely at these programs is that they tend to help students who would have gone to college anyway and are least likely to help students who are underrepresented on college campuses: poor students and students of color.[47] The Higher Education Act of 1965, which authorizes federal financial assistance programs, plainly states the point of financial aid: "to assist in making available benefits of higher education to qualified high school graduates of exceptional financial need." The usual politics that surrounds merit programs moves funds away from this goal. When faced with budget constraints, most states have tightened merit criteria rather than impose student or parental income caps to control costs—a move that strikes me as indefensible when most of the funding for state merit aid comes not from taxpayers but economically marginal people who invest their hopes in a lottery ticket.

Many institutions have tried to improve college access for low-income students. Between 1998 and 2011, sixty-nine highly selective institutions adopted "no-loan" financial aid policies to help low-income students afford college. Low-income enrollment at these institutions increased by 1–2 percent in the years following the policy change, for an average low-income representation in the student body of 10 percent.[48] Hill and Winston argue that low-income students should represent at least 12 percent of selective student bodies, roughly their share of the high-achieving applicant pool.[49] The Great Recession made this challenge more difficult. Since 2008, several selective schools have scaled back their aid policies. MIT, Dartmouth, Williams College, Wesleyan, and Cornell, to name a few, all decided to be less generous.[50] To minimize demand for financial aid, Grinnell College announced plans to recruit more wealthy students.[51]

Like every other sector in the global economy, colleges, even elite ones, have been buffeted by new realities in the marketplace. Boomer parents who lost life savings or jobs in the recession can't or won't pay high tuitions. Even those who can afford it blanch at the idea of paying $48,000 a year for a non-elite college. For all colleges, tuition revenue depends upon public perceptions of reputation and quality that are skewed by *US News*' insistence on rating schools by how well prepared students are when they enter. This puts tuition-dependent institutions that lack hefty endowments, which is most institutions, in a bind. They must balance their most democratic educational aims against the need to enroll sufficient numbers of students who raise SAT/ACT medians and are relatively better able to pay.

As Vassar president Catherine Bond Hill, an ardent advocate of socioeconomic diversity at her own institution, put it: "We have spent unsustainable amounts from our endowment and cut other costs during the recession in large part to meet these financial aid needs. . . . But higher education alone can't solve the affordability [dilemma]. Renewed government support is . . . essential."[52] Despite their loftier aims, the chief concern of higher education is not social equity but institutional viability. The leaders in higher education look to leaders in federal and state government for more help in financing the real costs of college or to fix the problems and inequalities that pervade the K-12 pipeline. That, however, presumes a much fairer politics than the broken, upward-redistributing one we have.

To its credit, the College Board has begun sending information packets to low-income high achievers, modeled on Hoxby and Turner's experiment, which will raise demand for financial aid at selective colleges. Hill predicts this is going to create tension, presumably between the class of students who are currently getting aid and those who are not. "About two-thirds of America's top 150 private colleges and universities with the highest endowments per student are not need-blind in admissions and already reject talented low-income applicants because of students' financial need," she wrote in a letter to the *New York Times*. While they are waiting for the federal government to give them more incentive to focus on actual financial need, perhaps these well-endowed places will reconsider whether they need any more fancy amenities to woo full-paying students or whether president and administrator salaries and the number of administrators might be reduced, among other possible strategies to reduce cost and raise need-based aid.

At minimum, universities should resist the hegemony of *US News*. The company gives no weight to diversity of any kind in its popular annual "Best Colleges" rankings.[53] Although it now publishes separate rankings for ethnic and racial diversity, the company takes no responsibility for its own role in discouraging colleges from being more socioeconomically diverse through a ranking system that prioritizes inputs that track wealth. Peter Conn, an English professor at the University of Pennsylvania who is exasperated by *US News*' "pernicious influence," argued at a public forum that "college administrators should get together and demand that [it] include economic diversity somewhere in its algorithm."[54] Apparently that has not happened, although a growing cadre of schools subverts the College Board, ACT, Inc., and *US News* somewhat by making standardized tests optional.[55]

Meanwhile, working-class whites are as alien as the children of the ghetto on selective college campuses and anti-intellectualism and denigration of "liberal elites" has become a common cultural sensibility among blue-collar whites or those who would lead them. There is a breach, a cultural chasm. All too often, disappointed white applicants turn their ire toward affirmative action and assume that a less-qualified racial minority took their spot. But the demand for optical diversity will continue long after affirmative action is dead. The imperative of optics makes it more likely that low-income or less advantaged white applicants are competing with higher-income whites for entrance. And less advantaged blacks are competing with higher-income blacks, and so on. People of all colors are disadvantaged by current, exclusionary practices in higher education because of where they live or where they went to school, or because they are poor.

CHAPTER FOUR

Place, Not Race, and Other Radical Reforms

In the fall of 2013, a new freshman class arrived on Amherst College's pastoral campus. Forty-five percent of them were students of color and 23 percent received federal Pell grants. I asked Tom Parker, Amherst's dean of admission and financial aid, what it meant for nearly one-quarter of new students to come from families making $40,000 or less. He has been working in college admissions for over thirty years, and recalled his own entry to Williams College in 1965 as one of the poorest kids in his class. "A political science professor was giving a lecture. He was talking about working-class Italian Americans, and he kept saying 'they, they.' And my thought was 'It's not 'they,' its 'we.' [Italian-Americans] are not an alien species." He recalled his classmates not believing him when he said near the end of the month that he had run out of money and could not join them for their usual weekend excursions to all-female colleges in search of dates or future wives. "That kind of obliviousness is far less likely at a place like Amherst now," Parker said. With robust socioeconomic diversity, all students and the faculty who teach them learn how millions of Americans actually live.

Tony Marx, president of Amherst from 2003 to 2011, oversaw a dramatic rise in socioeconomic diversity during his tenure. I interviewed him from his current perch as head of the New York Public Library. "The dynamic changed fundamentally when black, Latino, and poor kids reached critical numbers on campus," he told me. "Once they felt respected and a full part of the college, all kinds of historical defensiveness went away. Black alums no longer had to come to campus to school kids on how to be black at Amherst." Marx also says that with greater diversity, the school's identity changed. Amherst began to boast proudly that it was both the best *and* most diverse liberal arts college in America.

Marx has thought a lot about the mission of higher education. A graduate of P.S. 98 and the Bronx High School of Science in New York City, he wrote his senior college thesis at Yale on Plato's Academy, exploring the role of education in society. He says working in South Africa in the 1980s, helping to found a school that prepared more than a thousand black students for university, was pivotal for him. "Learning in a diverse community may be the most important thing that universities do," he said, "because students can now get more content electronically." Parents can justify paying dearly for four years on a physical campus because there are few other places in American society where a young person can acquire the skill of interacting with and learning from people from all walks of life. Diversity is key to advancing the mission of universities because, Marx says, "we can't educate students in the twenty-first century without a mix. If all students come from the same backgrounds, they are going to learn less on substance and less on process"—that is, how to relate to everyone.

In this way, universities have a unique role to play in American society, Marx reasons. Out of self-interest, they must purse a more fulsome mix of students to educate well. He also argues that elite higher education has special obligations because of its disproportionate impact on society in producing the leadership class. "If America is to be true to the ideal of opportunity, it is particularly important that elite institutions lead the way," he said.

For Marx, leadership meant taking some risks. When he arrived at Amherst, the school was ranked number one among liberal arts colleges and enjoyed a nearly $1 billion endowment, which has since doubled. Such prestige and wealth creates moral imperatives, both he and Amherst's Parker argue. "Elite higher education should spend as much energy recruiting the very best students from schools and neighborhoods they've never gone to as they spend on fundraising," Marx said. He also argues that elite colleges and universities should partner with less selective institutions to create more pathways to mobility. Under his leadership, Amherst began to accept transfer students, mainly from community colleges. Those transfer students' GPAs were higher, on average, than that of other Amherst students.

When I questioned Marx about how fiscally sustainable a drive for more socioeconomic diversity is, he told me that those policies helped inspire the largest gifts Amherst had ever seen, including one unrestricted cash gift of $100 million. "When alums see their college doing more as a leader, they give more," he said. The complexion of Amherst changed as the school's tactics changed. But it never sacrificed being extremely selective. "We just expended enormous energy finding very talented students where they were," Marx said.

Tom Parker has worked for three presidents at Amherst and says all of them, including current president Biddy Martin, have been committed to diversity. It helps to be at a school with a history and culture of access. From its inception in 1821 as a place for the "education of indigent young men of piety and talents for the Christian ministry," Amherst had a charity fund that paid the tuition of poor students. "It's part of our DNA," says Parker. But a culture of access can be created anywhere. Parker offers six ingredients for what he calls his "cookbook for diversity": 1) commitment from the top to the bottom of the organization; 2) money; 3) getting recruited students on campus for a visit at the college's expense; 4) partnering with an opportunity program for low-income kids, like QuestBridge or the Posse Foundation; 5) a no-loan policy; and 6) being willing to give up about twenty composite (math/verbal) SAT points.

Because Parker and Amherst have been so very successful with this recipe, I will share some of his insights about each ingredient:

- *Commitment from the top to the bottom of the organization.* "This is indispensable," says Parker. "You can't have an enthusiastic president like Tony [and his predecessors and successor] and an ambivalent board." To be successful, Parker says a university needs complete institutional buy-in and enthusiasm about the goal of increasing socioeconomic diversity from the president, board of trustees, faculty, and students. At Amherst, Emory, Rice, and other universities that have made great strides, diversity becomes an integral part of the identity of the school and part of what attracts students, faculty, and support for the institution. Strong regional schools such as the University of Charleston, Rochester Institute of Technology, and Clarke University have also successfully enhanced economic diversity on their campuses.[1] Perhaps because it has had to contend with a ban on race-based affirmative action since 1996, the University of California system is a national leader in socioeconomic diversity, with 40 percent of its student population on Pell grants, including 34 percent at Berkeley and 36 percent at UCLA, its most selective campuses.

- *Money.* "Diversity is costly. You have to face up to that," says Parker. "If you are going to have 20-plus percent of students on Pell grants, financial aid must be an incredible priority. At Amherst we have the means. With a $2 billion endowment, you've got some obligation to do some good or you don't deserve to exist. Even in a year when we lost 28 percent of our endowment, we did not retreat on this commitment." Among the most competitive colleges, only 14 percent of students represent the bottom half of the income scale, a figure that has not increased over two decades.[2] Schools with large endowments are best able to take on more low-income students. But socioeconomic demographics vary widely across even well-endowed campuses. Princeton, with the largest per capita endowment in the country, had only 12 percent Pell grant students in 2012–13.[3]

- *Getting recruited students on campus for a visit at the college's expense.* "A student in Brownsville, Texas, who has never been to an airport is not going to get to campus on his own," says Parker. In a typical year, Amherst brings 350 low-income achievers to campus. Attending to the needs of many travel novices for a few days involves a military-like attention to logistics. It requires a commitment not just in money but also the labor and love of the entire admissions team. Says Parker: "You can't have a ghettoized [diversity recruiter] trying to do this alone. You have to have a diverse staff both racially and socioeconomically, so that the entire team is involved in this. One of the big mistakes admissions offices make is to marginalize the diversity recruiter, as opposed to making it an office-wide affair, an all-hands-on-deck enterprise. The people doing this work must also be well compensated and given an appropriate title and chance for development."

- *Partnering with an opportunity program for low-income kids, like QuestBridge or the Posse Foundation.* Amherst was one of three founding members of QuestBridge, a college opportunity program that uses nontraditional databases to identify low-income achievers. It is working a revolution in the way top colleges find talented students and spreading "college knowledge" to achievers from overlooked places. QuestBridge invites thousands of identified students to participate in programs that prepare them to apply to college and matches selected finalists with top colleges. In 2013 it had thirty-five college partners, including some of the best-known selective schools in the country, but also great institutions that low-income strivers may not know exist, like Grinnell College in Iowa, Scripps College in Claremont, California, Colorado College in Colorado Springs, and Trinity College in Hartford, Connecticut. Parker says QuestBridge's recruiting success comes down to two words that get a low-income striver's attention: "full scholarship." All of QuestBridge's partners agree to meet 100 percent of a matched student's financial need.

- *A no-loan policy.* In 2000, Amherst introduced its no-loan policy, as did Princeton the following year. Other schools soon followed suit, including my alma mater, Vanderbilt. Over seventy schools—from Appalachian State to Arizona State, the University of Illinois to the University of Louisville—now offer such policies, some only for low-income students. They are doing their part to reintroduce opportunity to our land and putting pressure on their competitors to do the same. "This is an instance where competition works toward the common good," said Parker of the no-loan movement.

- *Being willing to give up about twenty composite (math/verbal) SAT points.* Parker admitted to me that making standardized tests optional might be an appropriate option (more on that below). For those institutions that have not yet joined the SAT-optional movement, Parker says a school that wants to achieve robust socioeconomic diversity will sacrifice only about twenty median SAT points, or the ACT equivalent.[4] "We could fill our entering class with 480 kids with near-perfect SATs," he said. "If a school wants a whole class of 'academic 1's,' then stop talking about socioeconomic diversity. You have to choose one or the other," he said of the median standardized test scores that *US News* and the schools enslaved to its rankings weigh too heavily. In admissions-speak, an "academic 1" is a super achiever with near-perfect scores and grades. They are often accomplished wealthy kids who have been "shot out of a cannon" by highly intelligent, motivated parents, says Parker. They may have had access to a dozen AP courses and extraordinary educational advantages that are typically available only in wealthy zip codes. "A poor kid with a 700-plus math or verbal score is every bit as intelligent as the kids who rank as an academic 1," Parker says. He is willing to accommodate lower standardized test scores for poor applicants, but only for straight-A students who took the most challenging classes at their school.

WHAT IS MERIT?

My conversation with Tom Parker concluded on the issue that makes the affirmative action debate so fraught. He admits that with thousands of students vying for so few spots, there is a lottery-like dimension to admissions at hyperselective schools. Amherst puts a substantial number of academic 1's on its wait list, and he says that any institution serious about racial and socioeconomic diversity has "to be willing to make that sacrifice." Opponents of affirmative action will argue that the waitlisted super achievers are unfairly sacrificed, although Parker says they "do fine" because they will be accepted somewhere and likely will enter one of "10 to 20 places."

Since Amherst still uses standardized tests in its evaluation of applicants, I asked Parker what threshold score he looks for to give him confidence that a student can do the work at Amherst. To his credit, Parker clarified that an SAT or ACT score was only one piece of evidence in an entire file that his admissions team evaluates. They want the student not only to be able to do the work, but to thrive and contribute to the Amherst community. Although he admits some students with lower scores, a combined math-verbal SAT score of 1300, or its ACT equivalent, was a number that would give Parker comfort about a student's ability to thrive. He would need to see other evidence of grit, "of stick-to-it-ness," he said. "Reading the file of the accomplished wealthy kid is very easy. Reading the file of a low-income kid is more like detective work," Parker said.

As he described this search for clues, I got a better sense of the intangible qualities Amherst looks for. "Straight A's are nonnegotiable," he said of low-income applicants—a strong predictor of a student's potential to persist through the challenges that await them at Amherst. He also looks for students who took the hardest classes available to them. If there is an AP program, he expects a low-income admit to have taken those classes. He also evaluates carefully how a student approached Amherst's invitation to visit the campus. "Did they show up on time at the airport? Were they organized? Did they party while on the trip?" he said. They often look at what an applicant's siblings have accomplished as an indicator of the student's likely upbringing and character. "That is an interesting marker," he said. "We look for a significant adult in the kid's life who is going to offer support. What does the kid do when he returns home for Christmas, or when he gets discouraged?"

Parker admits that he is engaging in affirmative action for low-income white and Asian students in much the same way he does for well-qualified black and Latino applicants. He holds lower-income achievers to different standards because they will not have had the same advantages as more affluent applicants. At Amherst, "a poor white or poor Asian is every bit as attractive as a poor black or Latino kid. That is not the case at a lot of places," Parker said. For about twenty-five years, Parker asserts, higher education has made a commitment to racial diversity. "Collectively, we have not made the commitment to diversity for low-income kids," he concluded.

Perhaps Abigail Fisher and Abigail Thernstrom might feel differently about affirmative action if there were transparent evidence that whites were also benefiting from a relaxation of numerical notions of merit. (Historically, yes, white women were primary beneficiaries of affirmative action.) As I argue below, it is past time for the lessons of decades of affirmative action—about what makes for a great student who contributes to the mission of a university—to be applied to *all* applicants. Conceptions of merit and how whites feel about those conceptions vary depending on who benefits and who is excluded.[5]

I ask Parker how he would approach evaluating applicants if he could not consider race. He thinks that without race the number of black and Latino students in the entering class might drop by a third to a half, although he admits that he has some "proxy strategies" in mind that he has never tried before. He wasn't willing to divulge them to me, but as I ask about the SAT-optional movement he begins to talk in ways that are suggestive. He admits that had the *Fisher* case barred Amherst from considering race, the school might have decided to make standardized tests optional.

The threat of lawsuits is not the only reason to reconsider using standardized tests to evaluate college applicants. At schools that accord them too much weight, they perform a gatekeeping function, because performance on the test is tightly correlated with socioeconomic status. A recent analysis of College Board data conducted by the *New York Times* is revealing. Each year, the College Board collects information from students when they sit down to take the SAT. About two-thirds of them voluntarily report their family's income, and the College Board reports average scores for ten income groups. "On every test section, moving up an income category was associated with an average score boost of over 12 points," the *New York Times* reported.[6] A student from a family earning $20,000 a year averaged below 460 on each section—math, verbal, and writing—while a student from a family making $200,000 averaged 560 to 580 on each section. The chart accompanying the data plotted the average scores for each income category along rising colored lines, suggesting one side of a steep mountain ascending sharply at the top to a near-vertical peak. The biggest gains in performance came with a leap from the affluent to the super-affluent. Young people from families making more than $200,000 do better, on average, than those from families making $160,000.[7]

Socioeconomic status is the best predictor of academic success, no matter the measure of achievement. There are several possible explanations for this correlation between SAT scores and income. Sociologist Sean Reardon recently analyzed data from nineteen nationally representative studies and found that the achievement gap between students from high-income and low-income families has grown by 40 percent since 1960, and is now double the gap between black and white students.[8]

Researchers speculate that this growing divide reflects differences in parental time spent with children, the amount of money invested in their cultivation, and differences in what parents do when they spend time with their kids. Affluent parents spend nine times the money that poor parents do on their children's development, a divide that is likely to widen.[9]

Affluent parents are more likely to be married and low-income parents are more likely to be single, such that affluent children generally receive more parenting. Affluent parents also tend to confer innate advantages on their offspring by talking to them more and exposing them to novel environments and stimulating materials. By age three, an affluent child will have heard about 30 million more words than a low-income child.[10] One study found that poor children's brains are similar to those of non-poor adults whose prefrontal lobes have been damaged—an area of the brain that affects executive functions like working memory, cognitive flexibility, and language.[11] Affluent people also tend to buy their way into zip codes or private schools that afford the best possible education—rigorous curricula and pervasive college knowledge that raise the college readiness of all who are fortunate to enter these environments.

The affluent buy other advantages on the private market. In the arms race surrounding college admissions, a cottage industry of tutors, test preparers, consultants, learning centers, and so on that only the affluent can tap into has sprung up. Only 8 percent of lower-income students take a test prep course, while 78 percent of affluent students do.[12] Among all high school students, only a quarter engage in test preparation for college entrance exams. Researchers find that a student whose parents can afford $6,000 for private SAT tutoring will enjoy a significant advantage over students whose parents cannot afford to pay a private coach.[13]

One need only look at the example of South Korea to gain insights into what motivated parents of means will do to help their children compete. Unlike in America, there is limited variation in school quality and curriculum in public schooling in South Korea, so parents invest in private tutoring, so-called shadow education, to gain an edge. About 70 percent of South Korean children participate in this system, with tutoring reaching a crescendo in periods leading up to high-stakes college entrance exams that determine life chances. The children arrive exhausted at their regular school because they have been slaving away at a *hagwon* until the wee hours, prompting the Korean government to impose a curfew that bans private tutoring in metropolitan areas after 10 p.m. and to rethink the role of standardized tests. This practice of shadow private education, long ingrained in East Asian cultures, has emerged in West and Central Asia, Europe, North America, and Africa, and is increasingly provided across national boundaries via the Internet.[14]

As long as there are wealth inequalities, there will be socioeconomic achievement gaps on standardized tests. As with geographic segregation and the unequal allocation of high-quality K-12 education, intentionally or not, the SAT has become a tool for hoarding the resource of selective higher education, even as it is imbued with an aura of objective fairness. Those who don't score high, it appears, have only themselves to blame. And yet using standardized test scores as indicia of merit rests on the invalid assumption that all those who take the test have had the same educational opportunities, experienced teachers, and well-resourced classrooms.

In addition to the objection that it propagates wealth advantages, it is particularly problematic to call an SAT score merit when it has limited predictive power. The SAT predicts only about 20 percent of grade variance among college freshman, and not much else. It has no correlation whatsoever to university mission statements, unless a college is willing to rewrite its mission to say: "Our purpose is to preserve advantages of wealth and income in America." A study that followed three classes of Harvard College graduates over thirty years and measured success in terms of financial and career satisfaction and contribution to the community found that the most successful alumni had low SAT scores and came from a blue-collar background.[15]

One study suggests that affirmative action entrants, with their lower test scores, become the alumni that most exemplify universities' frequently stated mission of cultivating community leaders who give back to society. Researchers examined the careers of three generations of graduates of the University of Michigan Law School and found a negative correlation between "hard credentials" like LSAT scores and service activities of alumni. They also found that a test-centered approach to admission did not predict future success in the profession any better than the whole-person approach used for affirmative action candidates. All

Michigan Law graduates tended to succeed, although those with higher LSAT scores tended to provide less pro bono legal service and devote less time to serving as community leaders. As Professor Lani Guinier said of the study, it suggested that test-based admissions policies "reward people who then often fail to give back to society" and also "fail to identify those who in fact have much to give and do give."[16]

In college admissions, high school grade point average is a better predictor than standardized test scores, not only of freshman grades in college but also of four-year college outcomes. Although arguments can be raised against overweighting grades, using cumulative high school GPA to evaluate college applicants is a more legitimate measure of merit because it is a better predictor of likely performance throughout college, *and* it has less adverse impact on disadvantaged and underrepresented minority students.[17] A study that examined academic outcomes of students by race and gender at twenty-eight selective colleges found that "the biggest effect in predicting college grades is that associated with high school GPA, whereas the SAT score is nowhere to be found among the strongest predictors."[18] The researchers concluded that this finding supported putting greater emphasis on grades than test scores not only in the selection of minority applicants but for *all* applicants. After high school GPA, the second-strongest predictor of college grades was "academic effort," which led researchers to recommend not just deemphasizing test scores but also for admissions offices "to devise better ways of identifying scholarly dedication, work ethic, and a willingness to forgo recreation for academics."

But even a high school GPA, on its own, is not strongly predictive of college GPA and graduation rates. "At best, test scores and high school grades explain less than half the difference in college freshman grades, and are even weaker determinants of . . . graduation," conclude Georgetown researchers Anthony Carnevale and Jeff Strohl.[19] A task force charged with evaluating admission criteria and diversity in the University of California system recommended that UC should rethink its idiosyncratic eligibility requirements for this reason. It called for a student's eligibility to be determined based upon a broad set of achievements, evaluated against the specific educational opportunities that were available to the student.[20] UC Berkeley and UCLA have since adopted a holistic approach to admission that engages in such an individualized assessment of achievement, reducing the significance of grades and test scores while also considering obstacles the student had to overcome.[21]

For those who view this as a watering-down of standards, think again. Extant psychological research popularized by Paul Tough's important book, *How Children Succeed,* demonstrates that noncognitive traits—like resilience, self-control, and the ability to delay gratification and persist past disappointments and failures—are more critical to ultimate success than cognitive skills. This is what Tom Parker's detective work does. Resilience can't be tested for, but it can be discerned. Holistic, individualized assessment of an applicant's entire file, reviewing multiple indicators of achievement, is the best and fairest approach to selective university admissions.[22] Holistic review is just as important for affluent candidates as it is for poor ones. Tough explains that wealthy, coddled children are often deprived of opportunities to develop resilience because their parents insulate them from failure.

The *US News* rankings provoke an excessive focus on numbers and make institutions risk averse. In truth, the range of students who are qualified to enter selective higher education is *much* broader than the median test scores and GPAs reported to *US News* suggest. Carnevale and Strohl estimate that even among the most prestigious colleges, 85 percent of students with an SAT or ACT equivalent score of 1000 to 1200 would graduate, although these colleges tend to require scores above 1250 for admission. The 1250 score raises the likely of graduation to 96 percent, although this eliminates a large cohort of disadvantaged students who likely would graduate if admissions officers did the detective work to find the most resilient achievers in this group.[23] Tom Parker's 1300 threshold of comfort for Amherst is a risk-free number that he can afford because he receives so many applications from low-income achievers that meet the threshold.

The important point is that all institutions and all of American society should resist the idea that differences in test scores above a certain threshold suggest something meaningful. According to Carnevale and Strohl, college graduation rates vary little among those students in the top half of the SAT and ACT score distribution. Especially at selective colleges, they report, a difference of 100 points on the SAT matters little as a predictor of graduation. It certainly does not predict differences in career success after graduation. Instead, such score differences matter most in the competition for seats in an entering class, because that is what *US News* and far too many institutions have chosen to value. A student in the upper half of the SAT/ACT distribution increases his or her chances of graduating from college as the selectivity of the college increases. What is happening in higher education (and the K-12 system that precedes it) is an increasing stratification of resources such that those who don't get into selective programs are less likely to graduate, not so much because of their lesser talents and drive, but because they are in underresourced institutions.[24]

We can—and we must—undermine this system of separate and unequal opportunity, and not just for a relative few who will gain admission to selective higher education through a relaxation of numerical standards that otherwise exclude. As I argue below, replacing exclusionary practices in university admissions with fairer ones that better screen for students who will advance the mission of higher education would be a beginning of a necessary movement to fix what is wrong with K-16 education generally. We need to begin to repair the social contract and create an opportunity system in which getting ahead is not a zero-sum competition with few winners. We can start by imagining a country where one's life chances in the economy are not tied rigidly to rankings, and where access to high-quality educational content and teaching does not turn on having money, so that we unleash the promise of all Americans and of America itself.

A final reason to rethink standardized tests and grades as the sine qua non of merit is what this rat race is doing to American youth. In K-12 education, in no small part because of the mandates of the No Child Left Behind Act, standardized testing is the means by which we evaluate student achievement. Few of our international competitors require children under sixteen to take standardized tests, and the United States has fallen in international rankings in education since NCLB required annual testing in grades three through eight and again in high school. In Finland—a country whose children regularly rank near the top in math and reading on the international Program for International Student Assessment, or

PISA, standards—children do less homework than American children do. They take almost no standardized tests and escape rote learning. They achieve academically *and* they are happy. Among other things, Finland invests more resources in lower-opportunity schools and has made teaching an elite profession that only the highest achievers may enter. Finland has figured out how to achieve its Finnish Dream.[25] We need to figure out how to restore our American one. But again, that presupposes a saner politics where government and institutions allocate resources fairly to bring all people along.

Affluent children will enjoy built-in advantages under any standard for college admission, so why put them and others who must compete with them through the stress of extreme emphasis on test scores and grades? I think of Sarah Rodeo, who told a *New York Times* reporter that she "cut out sleep" during her junior year to eke out more time to cram for the SAT and ACT and went into therapy to deal with her anxiety about her math performance. She devoted a year to test prep and noted that many of her classmates at the Hewitt School in Manhattan took a mock test every weekend.[26] I also think of the five suicides at a high-performing Palo Alto high school in 2009 and the one-fifth of American teenagers that are estimated to be depressed.[27]

Critics of this trend, which is making test preparation the primary junior year extra-curricular activity, point their fingers at parents who prize high-status colleges. I think they should blame the colleges that require these tests. *(A note to subversive college administrators: if you make standardized tests optional, your school might actually rise in the* US News *rankings.)*

Hopefully, we will soon reach a tipping point where institutions and the people who love them throw off the oppressions of rankings and throw a hammer to the whole admissions process and start breaking things—as did Bard College when it offered applicants the option of submitting four 2,500-word essays and no grades or test scores. Hopefully K-12 schools, higher education, and parents will begin to reject unfair nonsense and restore common sense that is good for students and promotes real learning. Imagine if we freed young people to develop a love of learning and allocate the useless hours spent on SAT/ACT preparation to extra sleep and their own passions. Imagine a country where over a million children did not drop out of high school each year in part because society promotes a narrow conception of success—a pyramid-like path to selective higher education—that only a relative few can enter. Enough.

THE PROBLEM WITH RACE

Proponents of race-based affirmative action argue that without it, the numbers of blacks and Latinos at selective schools will plummet. This has been the initial pattern in states that have banned use of race in admissions. In a study of five selective law schools in California, Texas, and Washington, enrollment rates initially declined by nearly two-thirds among African Americans and nearly one-third among Latinos.[28] Similarly precipitous declines in black enrollment have occurred at selective public undergraduate institutions immediately after a ban of affirmative action has taken effect. Black and Latino undergraduate enrollment at UC Berkeley fell by half immediately after the voter-approved Prop 209, which banned affirmative action in public programs, took effect in California.[29]

The picture is better when the lens is widened. A recent study of the impact of affirmative action bans in four states (California, Washington, Texas, and Florida) found that total enrollment of unrepresented minorities did not change at four-year universities. The decline occurred at *selective* schools, with black and Latino enrollment falling 4.3 percent overall at those schools.[30]

And yet some degree of diversity has endured, even in the wake of bans on the use of race. In California, demographic change alone is raising the numbers of Latinos attending college. Among Golden State residents admitted to the University of California system for the fall of 2012, 36 percent are Asian American, 28 percent white, 27 percent Latino, and 4 percent African American (in a state that is roughly 14 percent Asian, 40 percent white, 38 percent Latino, 7 percent black, and 4 percent multiracial). Of course, diversity's proponents would like to see better representation of African Americans and Latinos. In the *Fisher* case, leaders of the UT and UC systems filed briefs arguing that they could not achieve critical levels of diversity in all classrooms without consideration of race.

Yet, as I have argued, admissions officers can use race-based affirmative action to achieve optical diversity, admitting those applicants of color with a socioeconomic background not unlike that of applicants who gain entrance without the benefit of affirmative action. Race can make institutions complacent and unwilling to rethink exclusionary practices that are not relevant to mission. A system that enables elites of all colors to retain privileges and lock out those not rich enough to access selective K-12 education or expensive tutors and test preparation does not live up to our professed ideals about fairness.

Given the strong public opposition to use of race in college admissions and the risk of legal challenges under the tightened *Fisher* standard, it would make sense to tailor affirmative action to those who are actually disadvantaged by structural barriers, rather than continue with a race-based affirmative action that enables high-income, advantaged blacks to claim the legacy of American apartheid. For many but not all black youth, those disadvantages include exposure to concentrated poverty in segregated schools and neighborhoods and the deprivations of low family wealth. Research shows that low net worth affects a family's ability to purchase a home in a high-opportunity neighborhood with good schools, and it affects a student's confidence that working hard will enable her to attend college.[31] Another disadvantage disproportionately endured by native black children is growing up in single-parent households, with less child supervision and support than are typically available in two-parent families.[32] Richard Kahlenberg has argued that building these three elements of disadvantage—exposure to concentrated poverty, low wealth, and single-parent household status—into a disadvantaged-based affirmative action program would fairly consider factors known to affect educational outcomes while also disproportionately benefiting students of color.[33] I agree, but, as described below, I would give special primacy to place and other radical reforms that scrub the admissions process of unnecessary exclusion.

Such a design would answer critics of race-neutral, class-based affirmative action plans who argue that such programs favor whites who, regardless of economic status, do not have to deal with accumulated restrictions of race. William Julius Wilson has stated that he supports class-based affirmative action but does not view it as a substitute for race-based affirmative action because middle-class black kids often suffer the restrictions of segregated neighborhoods, and our racial history can make a black family's hold on middle-class status more fragile.[34] Wilson and others are correct in their assertion that mere consideration of income differences does not adequately reflect the structure of disadvantage in the United States. It is not enough to promote affirmative action based upon class rather than race when there is a racialized, separate and unequal K-12 pipeline. As noted earlier, low-income whites tend to be less economically segregated than affluent blacks. On average, they are less exposed to concentrated poverty and have a higher probability of living in middle-class settings that offer genuine opportunity and better schools. That said, whites who *do* live in impoverished environs or attend high-poverty schools are no less deserving of special consideration—as is anyone who is actually disadvantaged by economic isolation. If a middle-class black applicant is disadvantaged along some dimension other than place, as I argue below, a holistic approach to admissions would enable consideration of such actual disadvantage.

Recent research on disadvantage-based affirmative action that considered a complex range of factors beyond parental income, including parental education, language, neighborhood, and high school demographics, found that such programs would raise African American and Latino enrollment nearly as much as race-based affirmative action while also increasing economic diversity.[35] As Tony Marx told me, when Amherst dug deeper into the well of low-income talent in the United States, the racial and ethnic complexion of Amherst changed. A recent analysis of ten universities that adopted race-neutral plans found that at seven of them the representation of black and Latino students met or exceeded levels the schools had achieved with racial preferences.[36]

If we are honest about the extant data on the effects of moving from race-based to disadvantaged-based methods of affirmative action, the debate is really about how and whether African Americans will retain a meaningful presence at the most selective colleges and universities. (I deeply regret that Native Americans are invisible in this debate, largely because of a lack of reported data about them.) The most elite institutions in California's system of public higher education—UC Berkeley and UCLA—have yet to recover fully from Proposition 209 in terms of representation of black students, while they currently meet or exceed the numbers of Latino students they had under a race-based system.[37]

Among civil rights advocates, a familiar justification for continued use of race in college admissions is that it remains necessary to ensure the leadership class that emerges from very selective private and public institutions is diverse. In the *Fisher* case, UT's lawyer asserted during oral argument that it was important to be able to give extra consideration to a hypothesized son of a black dentist from a Dallas suburb. Mr. Garre reasoned: "[T]he minority candidate who has shown that . . . he or she has succeeded in an integrated environment" and has shown leadership and community service "is precisely the kind of candidate that's going to . . . come on campus [and] help to break down racial barriers, work across racial lines, [and] dispel stereotypes." Such candidates seemed more desirable to Garre (and possibly UT's admissions officers) because, he stated, "the minorities who are admitted [under the Ten Percent Plan] tend to come from segregated, racially identifiable schools."[38]

As a passionate advocate for integration, I believe in the value of diversity and the idea that people should be exposed to "the other." Still, there was something unseemly about UT's argument, as Justice Alito pointed out in his rejoinder: "Well, I thought the whole purpose of affirmative action was to help students who come from underprivileged backgrounds, but you make a very different argument that I don't think I've ever seen before. The top 10 percent plan admits . . . lots of Hispanics and a fair number of African Americans. But you say . . . it's faulty because it doesn't admit enough . . . who come from privileged backgrounds."[39]

UT, unlike its elite private competitors, has a surfeit of "minorities" from "segregated" communities because of the operation of a plan that admits the top 10 percent of every high school class. Unvarnished, their logic appears to be that they want to be able to compete for the most palatable or assimilated of black and brown students. This argument is just as unseemly as the fact that the primary beneficiaries of affirmative action at the nation's most selective private institutions are those that are most advantaged by parental education, neighborhood, or school quality.

Law professor Randall Kennedy ardently defends this consequence of affirmative action in his most recent book, *For Discrimination*. "[T]he single most powerful argument in favor of racial affirmative action is that it seeks to rectify . . . injuries that continue to put certain racial minorities at a competitive disadvantage with white peers," he writes.[40] While not his only argument, this "[m]aking amends for past wrongs" is achieved by affirmative action that benefits advantaged minorities, Kennedy reasons, because the most talented students of color will, in theory, help less-fortunate minorities. The problem I have with this logic is that there are *present* wrongs endured by disadvantaged kids of *all* colors and, with effort, institutions can find well-qualified disadvantaged students who are perfectly capable of competing, uplifting themselves, and being leaders. Where many see weakness, I look at the honor students from low-opportunity neighborhoods and see profound strength.

Let's face it, jettisoning race-based affirmative action will have costs. Fewer African Americans will gain entry to elite institutions under a system of diversity based upon structural disadvantage. This begs the question whether the marginal benefits of getting more blacks into elite institutions—for example, an 8 percent black class using race versus a 4 percent black class using other criteria—is worth the political costs of continued racial division. I think not. Not when the harms that flow from a racially divided electorate include mass incarceration and underinvestment in public education and the social safety net, among other potential consequences. Not when losing the tool of race will force institutions to adopt better, fairer admissions practices that will widen the pipeline to higher education for everyone, *including* middle-class black students. Even arch critics of the stratifications in higher education admit that "affirmative action is not enough to make more than a dent in the larger systemic racial and class bias[es]" that animate K-16 education, that it helps those who "overcome the odds, yet does relatively little to change the odds."[41]

In any event, if I am correct in my prediction that law and politics will continue to erode use of race-based affirmative action, it would make sense to get started on race-neutral reforms that have the potential to create real diversity and more social cohesion. I prefer strategies that will render centers of learning more racially and economically diverse while *encouraging* rather than *discouraging* cross-racial alliances. The Texas Ten Percent Plan emerged from a cross-racial coalition of black, Hispanic, and rural white members of the Texas legislature who represented districts that were not sending large numbers of students to UT institutions. The

Ten Percent Plan, however imperfect, guarantees admission to Texas' flagship public universities for the top 10 percent of all high school graduates. It opened up quality higher education to white, rural working-class strivers who were locked out under the conventional system. UT adopted a race-based affirmative action plan in addition to the Ten Percent Plan because it desired more racial diversity than that plan achieved. It would have been better to reexamine exclusionary practices that undermine the university's mission.

The Texas and Florida plans that send the top 10 and 20 percent of high school graduates, respectively, to state universities are imperfect alternatives that rely on racial segregation to achieve racial diversity by ostensibly race-neutral means. They are a beginning, and rare among diversity policies in that they account, albeit indirectly and incompletely, for the fact of residential segregation and its attendant disadvantages. California has also adopted a similar place-based program that guarantees admission to the UC system to the top 9 percent of graduates of each local high school. The UC system has also eliminated legacy preferences, as have some universities like Texas A&M and the University of Georgia.[42]

The University of Michigan is rare in that it has incorporated place—"residence in an economically disadvantaged region"—expressly into its diversity program design, although it is unclear what weight this factor is given in a context of holistic admissions review. UM also adopted geography-based scholarships as part of its strategy to increase racial diversity in a race-neutral way.[43] The fact that place has not played a more prominent role in the innovations that have been tried in states where race-based affirmative action has been banned suggests a lack of awareness of the way in which geography limits opportunity in the United States. For those most disadvantaged by segregation, beyond negative peer influences, less experienced teachers, less-resourced schools or violence, is the sheer stigma of being from a low-income area—biases that admissions officers may need to take affirmative steps to move past. After all, admitting middle- or upper-middle-class students of color is culturally much more comfortable and is likely to be less costly and less threatening to *US News* rankings than admitting inner-city strivers.

If an institution is sincere about achieving diversity and wishes to or is forced to do so without consideration of race, then giving special consideration to place is an important, underutilized, and fair tool. Place plays a role not only in creating academic achievement gaps between segregated black and Latino kids and others, but also in students' ability to gain marks of distinction that come more easily in resource-rich high schools thick with AP classes.[44] In the context of an admissions process that affords a holistic, individualized review of a variety of factors, extra weight should be given to living in a low-opportunity neighborhood (a poverty rate above 20 percent) or attending a high-poverty school. This would benefit those who most need and deserve affirmative action. It would also have the salutary benefit of encouraging racial and socioeconomic integration in low-opportunity neighborhoods. A strategic middle-class family might decide to stay in or move into a historically low-opportunity neighborhood in order to receive the benefit of this plus factor in college admissions.

I would not make place the only dimension for consideration of affirmative action, but I do think that, given how large it looms in structuring educational opportunity and outcomes, it should be given much greater weight and attention than it currently receives in diversity programs. I would also give considerable weight to another factor that disproportionately affects blacks and Latinos—low family wealth. I would characterize both of these forms of disadvantage—exposure to concentrated poverty and low family wealth—as "structural," because the racial dimensions of this disadvantage can be traced to intentionally discriminatory public and private policy choices that endured for decades.[45]

While single-parent status is another factor that disproportionately affects African American youth, the degree of government culpability in creating this phenomenon is less clear (and frankly beyond my realm of expertise). In any event, single-parent status and other forms of disadvantage can be captured in a diversity program that allows individual applicants to state what obstacles they have had to overcome. My point is that the structural disadvantages of segregation and low wealth should be given far more consideration and weight, on the order of magnitude currently given to race in race-based affirmative action programs. Affirmative action should be reserved for those of whatever color challenged by serious disadvantages. For those who are not, I think it is healthy to send a message that most global aspirants have already absorbed: rewards come to those who work exceedingly hard. In our bewilderingly diverse future, no one is entitled.

PLACE, NOT RACE, AND OTHER RADICAL REFORMS

The original purpose of affirmative action was to overcome the legacy of intentional racism. Most institutions and employers are no longer intentionally racist, and plaintiffs and advocates can invoke antidiscrimination laws and public opinion to fight racism where it does exist. The anti-racist rationale of affirmative action has been superseded by a generalized pursuit of diversity for its own sake. But fairness requires more. Given our nation's failure to live up to *Brown*, we have an obligation to acknowledge and ameliorate the injustice and damage of segregation—a moral imperative more important than diversity itself. Class-based affirmative action plans are insufficient to this task. Mere consideration of income differences among college applicants would not adequately reflect the structure of geographic disadvantage in the United States. Reforms to the admission process should be designed to mitigate the inequality in the K-12 pipeline *and* to help create the social cohesion needed to improve the pipeline.

If the American Dream is to be more than a platitude, the avenues to opportunity must be real, and universities have a unique role to play in countering the structural injustices that exist in our nation. Centers of learning may be the only remaining institutions in American society that are capable of transcending partisan gridlock to repair the social contract. In diverse, fragmented America, a widely shared value is the idea that no one should be limited in their access to opportunity or their pursuit of happiness on the basis of immutable characteristics like race, ethnicity, or nationality. Proponents and opponents of affirmative action alike invoke this ideal of equality, embodied in the Fourteenth Amendment, even if they do not agree on what such equality should mean in practice. The so-called American Dream, however tattered, is also premised upon equality among the classes. According to a favored shibboleth, all Americans, regardless of economic station, are supposed to be able to get ahead and prosper by dint of hard work.

A project of restoring the American Dream might begin with a principle of universal fairness based upon American values we profess to revere: freedom, opportunity, and universal human dignity. A true commitment to such ideals would require institutions and employers to rethink their traditional way of doing things, because existing systems are simply replicating and reinforcing socioeconomic advantage. This is contrary to the mission statements of most universities, almost all of which aim to serve the country and advance the whole of human knowledge. A country where the avenues to upward mobility are open mainly to the affluent contradicts the professed values of centers of learning.

In addition to an explicit use of place in any diversity calculus, I would consider a number of reforms aimed at reviving social mobility and the social contract in the United States. First, I would jettison the phrase affirmative action, with its loaded meanings. Most universities and employers have stopped using the term anyway, favoring an amorphous concept of "diversity" that does not require rethinking of existing norms that are in fact exclusionary. I prefer "diversity practice" because it conveys acceptance of the fact of a diverse society and the need, through daily effort, to create practices and structures that are truly inclusive. Colleges and employers should be forthright about how and why they value diversity, what diversity means to them, and the (fair) practices they undertake to achieve it. In this way, all comers will be on notice as to a given institution's commitments, and they can form realistic expectations or apply elsewhere. Being transparent about diversity commitments and practices will help promote actual fairness as well as a perception of fairness.

Second, institutions and employers should clarify their mission. Those institutions that are truly committed to diversity will explicitly incorporate that value into their mission statements. Then institutions and employers should *define merit in terms that are directly tied to advancing their mission*. Aspiring firefighters need to be able to demonstrate that they can deploy relevant technology to put out fires. A standardized test that merely performs a gatekeeping function and does not test for skills relevant to extinguishing fires is neither useful nor fair. The same could be said of most standardized tests. Universities must be willing to rethink ill-defined, exclusionary concepts of "merit." In my field of legal education, for example, among select law faculties the ability to publish theoretical articles in elite law journals is more valued than the ability to teach students how to practice law in the real world.

An institution truly committed to diversity and universal access to opportunity would make the SAT and ACT optional or not use it at all, as is the case at a long and growing list of hundreds of colleges.[46] It would not give special consideration to race, ethnicity, *or* legacy status. Instead, in addition to the standard application form, all applicants would be invited to submit an optional statement on what disadvantages they have had to overcome. All forms of disadvantage would be considered, but extra weight would be given to structural disadvantages like living in a high-poverty neighborhood, attending a high-poverty school, or low household wealth.

My argument about legacies is simple. Research establishes a correlation between parental educational attainment and student educational achievement.[47] Being the son or daughter of someone who has attended a university, especially an elite one, offers its own advantage. Legacy applicants are well prepared to compete. As with advantaged racial minorities, legacy applicants don't need or intrinsically deserve any special consideration.

Admissions office staff should be expanded in order to ensure that every applicant receives careful, holistic consideration of their individual application. Finally, financial aid should be based *solely* upon demonstrated financial need. The goal of the admissions and financial aid process should be to identify and support highly qualified applicants of all races and classes who personify the university's mission. The goal of society should be to delink success from the status of one's parents.

Admittedly, these ideas swim against a tide of entrenched practice and privilege. While many people complain about unfair racial preferences, far fewer voices engage with the evidence of de facto class preferences in university admissions. Professor Guinier is a notable exception.[48] If universities are unwilling to rethink conventional practices or reexamine what really counts as merit, as Guinier has suggested, an experimental lottery for some of the places in an entering class would be preferable to the current certainty of class advantage.[49] A university could define a baseline GPA and standardized test score that would be acceptable and let applicants roll their dice. At least then all strivers would have a modicum of hope, and systems would retain an aura of fairness.

None of the reforms I have suggested would trigger strict scrutiny from courts because they are race-neutral and designed to promote fairness and access for students of all colors, ethnicities, nationalities, and classes. These reforms are also much less likely to engender public opposition or lawsuits—although, yes, some legacy applicants and affluent people may whine when their built-in advantages are reduced. Other affluent people may welcome these reforms because they would expand rather than narrow the paths to a successful life, enable more students to bypass the drudgery of standardized tests, and enhance the possibility for learning on a truly diverse campus. Opinion polls suggest that voters would support giving a hardworking kid who has had to overcome attending a low-opportunity school a leg up in admissions.[50] This resonates as fair in a way that according a plus factor to someone by dint of skin color does not.

CHAPTER FIVE

Reconciliation

The Civil Rights Act of 1964 would not have become law without the support of House and Senate Republicans. President Lyndon Johnson partnered with Republican moderates who wanted to compete for black votes in order to overcome a filibuster by Southern Democrats intent on maintaining their way of life. That up is now down and few issues, much less civil rights, command bipartisan majorities should not deter visionaries from pursuing the common good. I begin this chapter with two parables that suggest a path to racial reconciliation for our nation. Both come from conservative "red" states and involve victories in legislatures won by a multiracial coalition that included Republicans. The first concerns diversity in higher education and a coalition that won new benefits for a rainbow of previously excluded students. In the second, a coalition succeeded in stopping a bill from passing that would have harmed a politically weak minority and damaged the state economy.

THE TEXAS TEN PERCENT PLAN

In 1997, Texas adopted a new law after the US Court of Appeals banned race-based affirmative action in *Hopwood v. Texas,* a case brought by four white applicants who were denied admission to the University of Texas School of Law.[1] The law guarantees admission to the public colleges and universities of Texas to graduating seniors in the top 10 percent of every high school in the state. The program, which was developed by a group of Latino and black activists, legislators, and academics, passed in the Texas legislature by one vote, after a conservative Republican rural member whose constituents were not regularly being admitted to the University of Texas decided to support the legislation.[2] As predicted, the plan increased minority enrollments and that of rural white students at the flagship public universities in the state.[3] Those students who gain entrance under the plan do so by class rank, not standardized tests or extracurricular activities that they may not have time or money to afford. The program has repaired one shred in Texas' social contract, forcing the same kind of trade-offs that robustly diverse private institutions like Rice University make in order to enrich their racial, geographic, and socioeconomic demographics.

The Ten Percent Plan ameliorates the effects of separate and unequal K-12 education by admitting high achievers from all places from which they apply. The law ended the dominance of a small number of wealthy high schools in UT admissions. And it changed the college-going behavior of high achievers in remote places that had never bothered to apply to UT Austin. Before the law was passed, 59 high schools accounted for half of UT's freshman class, among the 1,500 high schools in the state. By 2006, that number had nearly doubled. The impact was pronounced at UT Austin. Between 1996 and 2007, the number of feeder high schools to the flagship campus rose from 674 to more than 900. Researchers found that these new high schools were more likely to have large concentrations of minority students and poor white students and to be in rural areas or small towns and cities. They also found that once a high school experienced success in sending a student to the flagship, they continued to do so. The researchers surmised that one reason for the success in increasing applications from new places was that the Ten Percent Plan made transparent a previously opaque and unknown UT admission policy of accepting most students in the top 10 percent of their class.[4]

In other words, the Ten Percent Plan had the same effect as the tailored brochure that researchers Hoxby and Turner sent to high achievers in overlooked places. And the same effect QuestBridge has in eliminating confusion about the financial aid process by simply offering a full scholarship to low-income high achievers. All of these interventions helped high achievers from low-opportunity places understand that they could compete and access better opportunities.

The Ten Percent Plan has produced other important benefits. In addition to spawning similar laws in California and Florida, studies have shown that "Ten Percenters" outperform all other admitted students on all measures. Typically they have lower attrition rates, graduate in shorter time periods, and have better grades.[5] The end result is that affluent people concentrated in resource-rich school districts can no longer hoard an important public resource—the University of Texas—that is subsidized by all Texas taxpayers. And the plan has improved the quality and breadth of the pipeline to higher education in the state. One researcher found that the plan stimulated college-going behavior at schools that had weak college traditions. Student enrollment in advanced courses and attendance rates surged at high schools across the state after the plan was enacted. A state-sponsored scholarship program that encouraged students at disadvantaged high schools to attend UT and Texas A&M deepened these trends.[6] These interventions on behalf of students in disadvantaged districts likely would not have been created had the *Hopwood* ban not propelled the state to innovate.

Critics of the Ten Percent Plan point to the fact that it has caused some strategic behavior. One study found that as many as 25 percent of students intentionally choose a different high school in order to improve chances of being in the top 10 percent. Such strategic students tend to opt for a neighborhood high school instead of a more competitive magnet school.[7] I view this as salutary. It means that neighborhood schools are becoming more viable to more children, that college knowledge is being spread around because the most motivated students are not isolated in enclaves of advantage.

Despite this public policy success, parents in wealthy school attendance zones have repeatedly attacked the plan as unfair to highly qualified children in challenging schools that fall into the 11 percent or lower rank. After all, their kids are in a pressure cooker. In many cases, they have higher standardized test scores and have taken more AP classes than Ten Percenters from less advantaged schools. Parents raised their voices, and their representatives in the state legislature tried repeatedly to amend or repeal the plan, but the coalition backing the law has succeeded in thwarting those attempts for a decade. In the Texas House of Representatives, white Republicans from rural districts, blacks, and Latinos strongly support the existing program. They agreed to one amendment in 2009 whereby only UT Austin received some flexibility. That flagship campus can now limit Ten Percenters to 75 percent of its entering class, although it had sought a cap of 50 percent.

Republican Dan Branch of Dallas and Democrat Mike Villarreal of San Antonio brokered this compromise. The end result of a temporary ban on affirmative action in the late 1990s is a successful public policy that enhances opportunity across the state and a more cohesive politics—at least on the issue of access to public higher education in Texas. Members of a state legislature that rivals Washington, DC, for political gridlock have forged an enduring coalition for access that upsets the usual disproportionate influence of affluent suburbs on the state legislature.[8]

MISSISSIPPI IMMIGRANT RIGHTS ALLIANCE: "BLACKS + MIGRANTS + UNIONS = POWER"

In 2012, an anti-immigrant bill akin to those enacted in Arizona, Alabama, Georgia, and South Carolina, was defeated in Mississippi. Like others crafted by the American Legislative Exchange Council, this bill was designed to make undocumented immigrants so miserable that they would voluntarily leave the state. Supporters of the bill thought they would succeed because Republicans had taken control of both houses of the legislature in the November 2011 elections, for the first time since Reconstruction. In the same elections, Tea Party–backed Republican Phil Bryant was swept into the governor's mansion on a staunch anti-immigrant platform. The state Legislative Black Caucus kicked into action. In the previous decade it had defeated over two hundred anti-immigrant bills. But these black Democrats were no longer part of the controlling majority and therefore didn't command the committee chairs that had enabled them to defeat many measures. Instead, they used their voices to illustrate the ugliness of HB 488. "We forced a great debate in the house, until 1:30 in the morning," said Caucus leader Jim Evans to the *Nation*.[9]

Among its more odious provisions, HB 488 required law enforcement to verify the immigration status of people they arrested, inviting racial profiling. And schools would be required to report the immigration status of their students. Some black caucus members who had never weighed in on immigration spoke out against this attempted "ethnic cleansing." Many white legislators also rose to speak against the bill.[10] The lock-step ideologies that propelled anti immigrant measures in Georgia, Alabama, and South Carolina did not prevail in Mississippi because opponents in this particular Deep South state had organized.

Bill Chandler is the kind of culturally dexterous person white supremacists invented Jim Crow laws for. Racial categories and racial hierarchy were created in America not just to justify racial subordination, but also to separate "dangerous" whites from the people of color they might ally with.[11] Chandler is a white man, married to a black woman, who saw the need for an immigrants' rights organization to help undocumented Latinos in his state. He founded the Mississippi Immigrant Rights Alliance (MIRA) in 2000 because he was disturbed by police raids on immigrant homes and roadblocks to capture undocumented people in and around Jackson.[12]

Chandler and other leaders of MIRA calculated that blacks, who were 37 percent of the state population, joining forces with the citizen-children of undocumented Latinos, who were beginning to register to vote, and with union members would create a powerful political coalition "We wouldn't have had a chance against [HB 488] without 12 years of organizing work," explained Representative Evans to the *Nation*. Evans, who serves on MIRA's board, continued: "We worked on the conscience of people night and day, and built coalition after coalition. Over time, people have come around. The way people think about immigration in Mississippi today is nothing like the way they thought when we started."[13]

In 2000, MIRA began by organizing in workplaces with significant shares of both Latino and black workers, so that both groups would benefit. Chandler and his wife, L. Patricia Ice, and Evans held community forums in neighborhoods and tried to dispel the myth that immigrants would take away jobs from black folks.[14] They reached out to black state legislators for support, resisting the temptation to seek help from existing white allies because they knew they needed to do the hard work of building trust between black and brown people. They organized an annual "Unity Conference" to connect traditional black civil rights activists with organizers in the labor and immigrant communities. They put black civil rights activists and union officials on MIRA's board.[15]

The unions organizing in poultry plants, casinos, and factories where immigrant workers toiled were sympathetic to MIRA's agenda. While blacks, immigrants, and unions coalesced as core members of MIRA, employers were also tactical allies in defeating HB 488. Undocumented workers wanted to keep their jobs just as much as employers wanted them to work. When HB 488 was being debated, union locals—the food workers, catfish workers, electricians—sent members of all colors to the Capitol grounds in Jackson to protest. A congeries of church denominations, synagogues, *and* mosques sent their flocks. MIRA's decade of organizing and outreach culminated in a chorus of voices against tyranny born of fear, filling the halls of the Capitol.[16]

This swell of opposition made it easier for a conservative Republican to buck Tea Party orthodoxy. Lieutenant Governor Tate Reeves appointed rural Democrat Hob Bryan to chair the Senate Judiciary committee to which he assigned HB 488. The bill died when Bryan chose not to bring it up for a vote. Reeves issued a statement saying that he "respects the fact that the chairman listened to the concerns expressed by the Mississippi Economic Council, Farm Bureau, the Mississippi Poultry Association, and local cities, counties, police chiefs and sheriffs, about the impact of this bill on taxpayers."[17] Groups representing local government and law enforcement had sent a letter to legislators calling the law an "unfunded mandate" and decrying the cost to taxpayers of housing undocumented immigrants in local jails. It helped to see the dire effect neighboring Alabama's law had on its economy. This coalescing of strange bedfellows spared Mississippi further damage to its image, costly legal fees, dead crops, and lost business and tourist investment. Suddenly, the Magnolia State, the place that produces great writers and great blues could also be an exemplar—believe it or not—for racial reconciliation.

MIRA has remained vigilant in opposing anti-immigrant measures in the state. The coalition has also attacked voter ID measures, all racial profiling, and the war on drugs. Says Chandler of these efforts: "We need political alliances that mean something in the long term—permanent alliances, and a strategy for winning political power. That includes targeted voter registration that focuses on specific towns, neighborhoods and precincts."[18] MIRA uses these issues to engage citizens beyond just voting. It teaches people how to lobby their representatives and influence the legislative process.

As a new legislative session began, MIRA sponsored Civic Engagement Day in Jackson. Ordinary folks received an orientation about the legislative session, walked together to the capitol, held a news conference, and met with their legislators. They made it clear they wanted "No Arizona/Alabama style bill or any other anti-immigrant or racial profiling legislation in Mississippi!"[19] As they exercised basic rights of citizenship, not only to vote but also to agitate, they also gathered power. Frederick Douglass and Alexis de Tocqueville would have been proud.

A MIRA newsletter explained the purpose of Civic Engagement Day, and in doing so revealed its theory for building multiracial alliances. The newsletter said the anti-immigrant laws passed in other states

> violate our national values and national interests as well as our Constitution. They divide workers, promote racial profiling and deny equal justice. They are bad for business and our economic recovery, as similar laws enacted in other Southern states have bankrupted farmers and manufacturers and driven away corporations looking to locate there. They divert precious law enforcement resources away from public safety. They embolden white supremacists, as hate crimes against immigrants, and people of color are on the rise.[20]

In other words, MIRA speaks to common values and common harms.

THE THEORY AND PRACTICE OF
MULTIRACIAL ALLIANCE

Stokely Carmichael upset many whites and more than a few traditional civil rights leaders when he popularized the phrase Black Power in 1966. In a seminal book of the same name, he and political scientist Charles Hamilton wrote of coalition politics: "We believe that political relations are based on self-interest. . . . Politics results from a conflict of interests, not of consciences."[21] Pioneering organizer Saul Alinsky also insisted that the only basis on which long-term stable organizations could be built was the self-interest of their participants.[22]

Alinsky founded the Industrial Areas Foundation, whose affiliates follow the same principles. In more than twenty states, IAF's fifty-seven affiliates have organized local coalitions of institutions—usually churches, but also unions, education associations, and other groups. By focusing on institutions, IAF tries to avoid the ebb and flow of members that occurs when organizing people, since people get tired, move, or die. Institutions are more stable and provide a consistent, larger base of financial and human support. IAF affiliates draw from all racial, ethnic, and income groups in their respective metro regions. They also give poor and working-class people a real voice, training them to be leaders for their community. IAF affiliates tend to focus on practical solutions for community problems: issues that cut across potential racial divides, often involving schools, housing, youth, daycare, or transportation. Like Alinsky, IAF leaders frankly accept self-interest as the driving motivation for all parties involved in politics. Hence, IAF teaches its members how to identify self-interest and use it strategically. As a result, IAF affiliates often alter the political status quo and move policymakers to a better, usually more progressive course.[23]

Dallas Area Interfaith (DAI) is a prime example. Started by a group of black, white, and Latino ministers and local leaders, it transcends negative racial stereotypes by organizing around people's interests. By challenging the way certain public officials had been exploiting racial divisions, DAI was responsible for getting the city of Dallas, as well as the Dallas Independent School District, to create, and later increase, funding for afterschool programs throughout the school district. At the time, white and Latino members of the board operated as a voting bloc that frequently opposed what black members of the board wanted. DAI persuaded Latinos on the board to ally with black board members to support afterschool programs that white members had traditionally opposed but black and Latino kids desperately needed. After building trust among board members with this initial victory, DAI proceeded to transcend Dallas' "troubled racial politics" by organizing thousands of people to attend rallies and a hearing in support of a bond initiative that had been stymied. With the groundswell of support created by DAI, sponsors were able to raise the bond amount from $900 million to $1.4 billion. It passed overwhelmingly, in part because of DAI's get-out-the-vote campaign in the Hispanic community.

More recently, DAI mounted a vigorous petition drive and lobbying campaign to try to persuade the Texas legislature and Governor Rick Perry to accept federal funds offered under the Affordable Care Act to expand Medicaid coverage to the working poor. Nearly one-quarter of Texans do not have health insurance, the highest rate in the nation.[24] DAI members of all faiths and colors descended on the Capitol in Austin no fewer than seven times. They found some common ground with a Republican doctor in the House of Representatives; however, Dr. John Zerwas's compromise proposal did not win favor with Perry and archconservatives. Sometimes an activist's only victory is in mounting the fight. DAI did force a very public debate on Perry's decision to forgo $100 billon federal dollars over a decade that would have expanded coverage to more than 1.5 million working but struggling Texans.

William Julius Wilson is enamored of IAF and has argued that national multiracial coalitions could shift national policy into a permanent progressivism.[25] The IAF avoids direct discussion of race, preferring to focus on race-neutral issues and engage constituents based upon self-interest. It is effective in that local affiliates have brought about thousands of community improvements.[26] But arguments from self-interest are almost irrelevant to opponents of Obamacare. The obsessions that lead Republicans in Congress to shut down the federal government in a bid to defund the law, or that motivate Texas leaders to turn down free money, are ideological and counter to objective facts about what is likely to be in Texas' fiscal and economic interest.[27] As I discussed previously, social psychologists link much opposition to health care expansion to high levels of racial resentment. Again, I am not saying that opponents are racist, but that racial resentments and gaps of perception about who benefits from government programs animate current political divides.

Academics and policy wonks debate whether avoiding race is a good idea when trying to build interracial trust. Wilson argues, for example, that the proper strategy is not to avoid racially charged issues like affirmative action, but to reframe them as benefiting all races.[28] This is similar to the work of Lani Guinier and Gerald Torres. They argued in the *Miner's*

Canary that race, or the condition of the most marginalized racial minority, should be used as a diagnostic for understanding how some social systems harm everyone.[29]

Recent evidence from social psychology suggests why these strategies aren't likely to succeed. As I discussed in chapter 1, many white people believe blacks have only themselves to blame for not getting ahead. In the age of Obama, a majority of whites believe that we have achieved our racially egalitarian ideals at their expense. In an era of rising white resentment, when most people harbor negative racial stereotypes about African Americans, these biases often stymie commonsense public policies. Failing to recognize and directly counter these biases and perception gaps, then, will likely result in failure to garner a majority consensus, particularly on policies designed to reduce inequality.[30]

The most successful multiracial coalitions mirror academic and social science research about what works in breaking down barriers of race. A message and program that taps into and reinforces most people's identity as nonracist is more likely to succeed.[31] Law professors john powell and Rachel Godsil underscore what social psychology research has revealed about the power of widely shared fundamental values. "To allow people to maintain a self-concept as egalitarian—but to challenge behavior and structural conditions that are inconsistent with those values—is the only route to progress," they argue.[32]

Processes and structures can be accurately described as racialized without suggesting that *only* people of color suffer the harms of these processes.[33] Actually, most nonaffluent Americans suffer the harms of racialized structures, including the challenge of accessing quality schooling and affordable housing, long commutes, the foreclosure crisis, the costs and consequences of mass incarceration, and gridlocked politics.[34] I am not arguing that race doesn't matter, as do advocates of color-blindness, or that race should be avoided for strategic reasons, as have some scholars.[35] I am arguing, based upon insights from social psychology, for much more care and intention in building alliances that transcend boundaries of racial identity.

Sometimes race must be discussed to build trust and form an agenda that is meaningful. When people are told that race may be salient, without language that suggests *they* are racist, they often attempt to conform to their egalitarian views. In studies of juries, for example, when issues of race are present, white jurors tend to treat black defendants more harshly than non-blacks. However, when white jurors are explicitly told about these risks, they treat black and white defendants equally.[36]

"Racism" may be the right word to use to describe a situation, but often it is sloppy overkill. Even if it is accurate as a descriptive matter, if building multiracial power is the goal, there are better ways to engage. Godsil and powell now use phrases like "structural barriers," "structural racialization," or "structural marginalization" where they might have used "institutional racism" in the past.[37] Consciously or not, white people may hear the word "racist" or "racism" as an accusation against them individually. Language is important. One can talk about the harm of systems and separate that from the individuals who must figure out how to make their way within these systems.

Social psychologists find that many whites are quite concerned that they will be "rejected by out group members."[38] Feel white people's pain for a moment. In interracial settings, they have to be so careful. Anything they say about race can and will be used against them if they err and say something that offends. They don't have permission to be merely ignorant or inexperienced on a subject. Their worst fear is that they will be perceived as a racist. The path of least resistance for them is to avoid race altogether. So if you want them to join your coalition, you have to reach out, invite them, and create a context and vocabulary in which they and you can work on something together that advances shared values.

Another reason organizing around common values and common harms is likely to be more effective than organizing around racial identity is that identity is fluid. A person can have multiple identities, with one becoming more salient depending on the context. When I drop my kids off at school, I am a mother. Most salient as I say goodbye is the love and joy that courses through me when that identity is primed. Race is tangential to that identity until the context changes or something triggers the mother-of-black-boys aspect of this identity. Woman, mom, wife, black woman, Christian, writer, professor—the identity strain that becomes most salient depends on where I am and what I am doing. Everyone has conscious or subconscious senses of in-groups to which they belong and out-groups to which they don't. Race will often be an inaccurate marker of what someone's perceived interest or values are in a given situation.

Whatever identities individuals perform, we need to transcend, to create new collective identities. To succeed, a coalition must incorporate some people who are not already with you—with the emphasis on *some*, not all. Coalition building is about getting to 55 percent or whatever number produces a win. At the local and state level sometimes a bare majority will do, unlike in Congress with supermajority requirements to overcome a policy filibuster in the Senate or Tea-Party bluster in the House. But in fractured America, if a coalition does not include some strange bedfellows, it is unlikely to succeed. The perception gap is too wide and too easy for deep pockets to exploit. Opponents of the common good now spend more money targeting and ousting incumbent Republicans who compromise than they do attacking Democrats.[39] In this environment, our only hope for promoting fairness and the common good is to reach the hearts and minds of more voters.

BUILDING ONE AMERICA, BUILDING ONE NEW JERSEY

Organizations like the Gamaliel Foundation and Building One America (BOA), which teach people how to build strong multiracial coalitions that can win state and local policy battles, do not shrink from discussing racial issues.[40] Building One New Jersey (formerly the New Jersey Regional Coalition), a BOA affiliate, is a statewide, grassroots coalition of local officials, faith leaders, and engaged citizens. They are committed to equity and inclusion and have won victories in the state legislature to protect fair-share affordable housing and equitable school financing. On the fraught issue of blocking affluent suburbs from contracting out of their legal affordable housing obligations through Regional Contribution Agreements (RCAs), Building One New Jersey never backed away from discussing race. Instead, it used race as a weapon, branding "the system" and never individuals as promoting and perpetuating segregation while offering an alternative vision of diverse, stable communities that could be model cities and suburbs.[41]

Paul Scully, executive director of Building One America and former director of Building One New Jersey (BONJ), shared a story with me about how transformative discussions of race can be. This tale is about Jim, a working-class guy, a barber, who was active in the local Democratic Party and in St. Jude Catholic Church in his town, Gloucester Township. The township is at the far southeast end of Camden County, about twenty minutes from Camden and Philadelphia. It is a classic blue-collar, white-flight community largely populated by South Philly Italians, Irish, Germans, and Eastern Europeans who "escaped" their old neighborhoods decades ago. Over the years it became much more diverse as urban movers of color also sought their suburban dreams.

Jim was floored when he heard Rick Taylor, then the African American mayor of Pennsauken, a neighboring suburb, speak at a BONJ event. Taylor talked about how he was actively recruiting whites to stay in or move to Pennsauken to try to maintain stable integration. Pennsauken was racially mixed but at risk of resegregating. Jim saw similar challenges for Gloucester Township and began to pester BONJ to bring Mayor Taylor to speak at his church. About 200 people turned out to hear Taylor give the same frank talk about race, integration, and community stability.

For Jim it was a revelation. "He wanted to talk aloud about race," said Scully. "He talked about how blacks and Hispanics were moving in and whites were moving out and how there were a couple of bad, high-crime subdivisions with too much Section 8 run by absentee slumlords." Scully told Jim that he should be very proud that Gloucester reflected almost exactly the demographics of the south Jersey metro region, not just in terms of race but also in the mix of income earners and variety of types of housing stock—rental apartments and detached houses, renters and homeowners. In every way, Gloucester Township was prototypical. "Congratulations on having one of the most racially and economically diverse communities in the state," Scully said to Jim. "Now what is your town's plan for keeping it that way?"

No one had ever thought, let alone talked about Gloucester Township this way. It is not Montclair or Maplewood—tonier New Jersey suburbs with a reputation for racial integration among the higher-income people who can afford to live there. BONJ and Rick Taylor had given

Jim a vocabulary for speaking forthrightly about how rapid racial change and pockets of concentrated poverty were undermining and destabilizing his town and schools—issues that the town never talked about publicly because there was no common language for discussing it. After Taylor's talk, Jim and others in attendance were energized. They built a multiracial, bipartisan base in Gloucester Township and recruited the town's Republican mayor, Cindy Rau-Hatton, who became one of BONJ's most important public champions in the statewide fight to stop RCAs.

In part because of Rick Taylor's leadership, Pennsauken decided to turn down a $3 million RCA payment from an affluent suburb because it concluded that it was unfair and fiscally unwise to concentrate more affordable housing in their town when a job-rich suburb was not taking on its fair share. Mayor Rau-Hatton agreed and had similar concerns for Gloucester Township. She testified before the state legislature and at press conferences along with black leaders from across the state about the evils of RCAs and their destabilizing impact on diverse communities. "The time has come for all municipalities to provide housing for low- and moderate-income citizens," she said. "It can only make our communities economically and socially balanced, and provide fair and equal opportunities for all residents."[42] "Say No to Evil! Ask Jon Corzine to take a stand against Jim Crow in New Jersey" read BONJ's more pointed flyer, cueing widely held values against racial injustice.

Scully said that for Jim, Mayor Rau-Hatton, and other whites in their coalition, this fight was one of the most moving experiences of their lives. Once they understood how their interests and values were being undermined by racialized structures, they were eager to join a multiracial coalition for regional fairness. BONJ helped spread this understanding through objective, geographically mapped data. Ultimately, BONJ was successful in defeating RCAs in the legislature. Scully says that Gloucester Township's involvement was decisive in helping BONJ win. It is one of the largest towns in the state and was not only middle- and working-class and racially diverse, but also politically mixed in one of the most competitive legislative districts in the state.

Bringing Gloucester into the BONJ fold was part of Scully's theory of "fault-line" organizing. He had paid attention to the work of Myron Orfield, a national expert on metropolitan politics and equity, who had analyzed the relationship between political volatility and racial change. Orfield found that diverse suburbs were often the swing districts that decided the outcomes of state and national elections and determined which party would control the state legislature.[43] BONJ invested heavily in Gloucester Township and some other fault-line places across the state where they were able to turn what others might have seen as a disadvantage of racial change to an advantage, claiming diversity as a positive and helping communities to value it and work at maintaining it.

THE HARD ISSUE

America desperately needs this work. A large majority of people say that they would prefer to live in politically, racially, and socioeconomically diverse communities.[44] However, even in liberal, Obama-leaning communities, residents who actually live with racial diversity express considerable ambivalence about it. This ambivalence leads them not to undertake significant steps as a community to maintain diversity.[45] Robert Putnam, professor of public policy and author of *Bowling Alone*, has found that people living in diverse communities tend to retreat from civic engagement.[46] Every place where racial change is occurring must confront this. Doing nothing, not talking about and addressing racial diversity openly, likely means ambivalence and instability will prevail. Without activism and organizing, social mobility will continue to erode, because civic engagement and the strong public schools such engagement fosters seem to be critical ingredients to making a place or region an engine of opportunity.[47]

This project of multiracial community building is difficult. Like a marriage, it requires work, compromise, negotiation, and a degree of consensus that will only come about with intentional effort. What we have now is a prevailing subtext of anxiety about race and racial change and a national politics set against compromise.

Not enough progressive groups do this intentional work. Advocates of economic fairness and racial justice often don't confront squarely what must be done to create a politics that might lead to more fairness. Demographic change will help. Voter registration drives will help. But only reconciliation, direct attempts to ally with reachable whites who hew Republican, will create a true politics of fairness. MIRA advanced its cause by being clear about who the "true villains" were, "the less visible forces undermining economic security for all low-wage workers."[48] They work overtime at getting people of different skin colors to recognize that they are struggling against the same forces, even as they are impacted in different ways, and that their beef is not and should not be with each other. That message has to be the basis of unrelenting outreach that continues, year in and year out.

Another key to the victories of MIRA, Texas' Ten Percent Plan coalition, and BONJ was that their causes tapped into universal values of fairness, like the civil rights movement itself. In his letter from a Birmingham jail, Dr. Martin Luther King Jr. wrote of the "inescapable network of mutuality"—the idea that injustice in Birmingham was a threat to justice everywhere else. For King, segregation was not just "politically, economically and sociologically unsound," it was "morally wrong and sinful."[49] This absolute clarity about moral rightness and wrongness was critical to the success of the movement. King was a tactician who sought to arouse the conscience of a nation. The means—nonviolence—had to be as just as the end. It took moral imagination in 1963 to envision an integrated society premised on universal human dignity. Youth today study pre–civil rights America and don't recognize their country. Perhaps fifty years from now, future youth will look back on America after the Great Recession, with its dream-killing stratifications, and wonder: how, why?

With effort, strange bedfellows can unite against unfair structural barriers even if those systems distribute burdens unevenly. White rural, white struggling suburban, black inner city, black middle class, Latino barrio, Latino middle class, Native reservation, urban Indian, poor Asian— all of these people are hurt by geographic concentrations of wealth and resources to different degrees and in different ways. Even affluent people living in high-opportunity places suffer harms of socioeconomic stratification, although they may not connect the dots.

Getting progressive non-whites to acknowledge white suffering will be a challenge. So much civil rights discourse leads with the fact of racial disparities, even though many whites are also oppressed by plutocratic arrangements. Yet struggling whites are usually invisible in civil rights advocacy. Racial disparities exist. They are relevant for assessing progress.[50] They are not the right point of entry for multiracial coalition building because many whites hear in them an accusation of racism (i.e., it's the white man's fault) and of exclusion (i.e., my economic pain is irrelevant simply because I am white). A language grounded in the history of racial discrimination and its legacy will no longer do. A language that acknowledges present structural barriers that people of all colors endure is critical to building power.

Just as for many people of color, systems of social mobility are not working well for working-class whites. A disproportionately large percentage of young, working-class adults who, according to their test scores and grade point averages, could attend college are not doing so or are failing to graduate. They are relegated to a life of economic struggle, and, as Thomas Edsall argues, there is "a reservoir of resentment over this state waiting to be tapped by either party."[51] But growing racial complexity will make it easier for politicians and political parties to exploit racial fears of still-dominant white voters, or of any voter who may harbor misgivings or worse about a different demographic group. This is the signature challenge that exploding diversity presents for American democracy in the twenty-first century.

Think about it. Struggling white people have few places to go with their anger and frustration. They can't celebrate their whiteness or organize around it, lest they be rendered social pariahs. The closest proxy for their economic interests has been the labor movement, which has eroded dramatically and is attacked by both the GOP and the Tea Party movement. So they gravitate to the GOP or the Tea Party, I suspect, because these are cultural homes where they feel valued and included. Progressive politics has declined as the labor movement and local machine politics have declined, the result of a loss of local institutions committed to economic fairness that can mobilize people.[52] In 2012, working-class households with a union member were more likely to vote for Obama than those without one; researchers speculate this is because unions impart facts about actual self-interest.[53] The political movement or coalition that wins these voters must have an organization that connects with them individually.

Whites who are shut out of the traditional avenue to middle-class status—college—are most disgruntled and susceptible to race-baiting. This is one reason I propose to replace race with place in affirmative action, along with other reforms to eliminate unfair structural barriers in higher education. In addition to making place a fulcrum for distributing access to higher education, place is also a good framework for organizing. Much of America's middle class now lives in suburbs that are global in their demographics and gaining population faster than more affluent, predominately white suburban enclaves.[54] African Americans, Latinos, recent immigrants from Somalia to Singapore, and middle- and working-class whites who live in diverse suburbia are all seeking opportunity, the chance to create and maintain a middle-class life. As I described in chapter 2, some of these places contend with increasing poverty, struggling schools, aging infrastructure, and a declining tax base. Yet diverse suburbs also tend to feature bipartisan civil debate, and they have more independent voters and more competitive election districts than other places. Partisanship may have reached toxic levels in Washington, DC, but in these places it is still possible to create a functional regional politics for fairness and begin to create and sustain diverse local utopias.

If you want to find a white coalition partner for regional fairness, look in a place that has been ravaged by the global economy: Where factories have closed and middle-class jobs have evaporated. Where schools were once very good and are struggling to stay that way after a rapid increase in poverty. Where food pantries have long lines. If you assume you can't work with blue-collar white folks or a Republican who represents them, you will continue to lose whatever policy battle you are fighting. Find those whom you can work with, who have constituents with values and problems similar to yours.

I am not writing about electoral coalitions. Although necessary, they are one-shot arrangements that tend to dissipate after the election is over and depend on the charisma of the candidate and his or her organization. I am writing about the much more important work of building a multiracial coalition that endures and holds elected officials of both political parties accountable; that returns citizens to their rightful place in democracy, not just as voters and taxpayers but also as people willing to lobby representatives and demand to be heard; that changes politics to a better course responsible to the will of the people, not to deep pockets that all too often sway outcomes.

There is nothing wrong with power, used correctly. Activists should not be shy about a goal of building political power. Call it a sanity alliance, if you will. I write this not as a cheerleader for the Democratic Party but as a citizen who longs for a functional democracy in which parties and politicians vigorously compete for votes from Americans of *all* colors. Democracy will have returned to America when ordinary people and the alliances that purport to represent them can make government or other relevant institutions responsive to their needs.

With demographic change and the rising cultural dexterity that occurs in spaces where no one group dominates, this work will get easier. Culturally dexterous people are the least prejudiced among us. I call them ardent integrators. They move toward rather than away from difference, and they accelerate the racial enlightenment of those around them, like the grandparents of biracial children. According to the first-ever National Survey of Adoptive Parents conducted by the federal government, 40 percent of adopted children are of a different race, ethnicity, or culture than their adoptive parents.[55] Evidence from the Pew Research Center suggests that interracial intimacy is poised to explode in America—from dating, marriage, and adoption to genuine friendship not of the Facebook kind.[56] Arguably, younger generations express and live more racial tolerance than do their parents because their demographic cohort is more diverse. Babies born today, America's first "majority-minority" generation, will create a multicultural milieu that Baby Boomers couldn't imagine.

This has profound implications for race relations and politics. Whites who have developed an enhanced capacity for interracial dealings are quite similar to people of color in their vision for this country. According to social psychology research, they tend to ground their perceptions about racial progress not to our success in dismantling Jim Crow but to a future ideal of full equality for all. They are apt to say in opinion polls, as do people of color, that more racial progress is needed, and they are more likely than less dexterous whites to support policies designed to promote diversity and reduce inequality.[57]

Social psychologists have also demonstrated that people with friends of another racial or ethnic group tend to be less biased.[58] In blunt statistical terms, with each passing decade, as the ranks of culturally dexterous whites and center-left leaning citizens of color swell, it will be easier for multiracial coalitions to get to 55 percent. Ardent integrators are replacing tired scripts about race. They willingly accommodate to difference and accept that in environs where no one group dominates, negotiation, collaboration, and sometimes compromise are required. With pervasive diversity, all institutions and individuals will be forced to undertake this emotional work, or risk irrelevance.

So find and join the most effective multiracial coalition in your state or community, dear reader. Or start one if it doesn't exist. Get to work on expanding its demographic reach and power. Don't be afraid to try and fail repeatedly. The activist, whether liberal or conservative, libertarian or proletarian, never gets to stop fighting for what she believes in. For now, our goal must be to unleash politics from the shackles of racial division.

Please be patient in this work. Social media cannot supplant the intensive labor it requires. When Bull Connor turned fire hoses and attack dogs on the children of Birmingham, nearly a thousand nonviolent protests erupted in over a hundred Southern cities, resulting in over twenty thousand arrests. While the shock waves of protest may have seemed spontaneous, they were the result of years of grassroots organizing. After the success of the Montgomery Bus Boycott of 1955, King and others formed the Southern Christian Leadership Conference (SCLC) in 1957 with the express goal of stimulating mass direct action against racial oppression. SCLC united Southern black ministers who had been involved in local protest movements. In his "Letter from Birmingham Jail," King refers to some eighty-five SCLC affiliates. They had established training institutions, like the Highlander Folk School, to cultivate local civil rights leadership across the South that would be skilled in the tactics of nonviolent social protest. The movement was founded on the persistent building of local institutions that could undertake similar training of citizens everywhere. The major cultural events of the civil rights movement—the Montgomery Bus Boycott, the Freedom Rides, the Student Non-Violent Coordinating Committee's Freedom Summer in Mississippi, and the Birmingham protests—all flowed from extensive, intentional grassroots organization.[59]

Freedom is not free. Real democracy must be paid for with sweat equity. There is no permanence in politics. There are only new battles to be fought, and new coalitions to form.

CONCLUSION

Fairness is the core American value. We fought a revolution to free ourselves from tyranny damaging to the pursuit of happiness, and we must keep fighting to make America fair for all. When the founding fathers declared their self-evident truths, they left to future generations how to render the lofty rhetoric of the Declaration of Independence true for slaves, Native Americans, women, indentured servants, and white men without property, almost none of whom could vote. In theory, all men were created equal, but in practice the founders sanctioned racial and economic hierarchy so that men of influence could come to agreement on a new national government. Founders like James Madison, a slave owner who feared redistribution, sought to temper the passions of the masses by allowing them to elect representatives "whose wisdom may best discern the true interests of their country."[1]

It would take nearly two hundred years for the founders' moral ideals to topple the edifice of supremacy they constructed. When the Supreme Court sanctioned slavery and the lowly, denigrated position of Africans in America in the *Dred Scott* case, Frederick Douglass responded not by attacking the Constitution or its drafters but by interpreting it in light of the Declaration of Independence. Its values and rhetoric bore the true meaning of the Constitution's drafters, Douglass argued. "We the people" necessarily meant all of "the human inhabitants of the United States," not only white people, not only citizens or legal voters or the privileged classes, but all men and women in the land.[2] Democracy necessarily involves contest. Douglass and other agitators fought for the founders' more capacious vision of universal human dignity. He could see past the darkness of his times and chose the constitutional interpretation that proved more enduring and fit with our highest ideals.

Abraham Lincoln reaffirmed this founding principle of universal equality in the Gettysburg Address. The best way to honor the Civil War soldiers who died for this principle was "for us the living" to continue their "unfinished work," so that government of the people would not perish. Civil rights revolutionaries also died for the same cause. Because of their work in Birmingham, Selma, and beyond, our founding ideal is now a widely shared value. However, like each generation before us, it is our turn to reinvent America, to redefine its race relations anew so that this cherished value of equality might be true for most people in their daily lives. We have to organize so that our institutions actually reflect our values.

Systems are rigged against all middle-income and poor people. Performance on the SAT mirrors family income. Access to an excellent public school depends heavily on your ability to buy your way into an affluent neighborhood. Access to employment depends on who you know and having skills that you may not be able to afford to acquire. Even those middle-class people blessed with a regular paycheck, health care, and a sound roof over their heads struggle to form or raise a family in a way that prepares the next generation to prosper. Social mobility in the "land of opportunity" has ground to a halt. Meanwhile, without a strong multiracial majority, there is little chance of enacting sound policies that might correct the underlying structures that create racial and economic inequality. In the case of extreme gerrymandering and super-majority requirements to break a filibuster on a policy debate in the US Senate, even more cross-racial political cohesion is required.

Nothing will get better, then, without reconciliation between sizeable numbers of whites and people of color. There are plenty of commonsense ideas about how to create more, not less, opportunity in this country. What we need is a politics of fairness, one in which people of color and the white people who are open to them move past racial resentment to form an alliance of the sane. The sanity alliance might get some things done for the common good of all of us.

We can begin to reconcile, to move past racial resentments and create a politics of fairness, by being quite intentional in our choice of policies and language. One first step would be to base affirmative action upon structural disadvantage, not race. Working-class whites need a clear signal that they are welcome to enter the multiracial tent, and this would be one such signal.

However, jettisoning race-based affirmative action is the beginning, not the end, of creating a fairer society. While we should not favor one race over others for preferential treatment, we also should not single out one group over others for discriminatory treatment. That, too, is un-American. Mass incarceration and racial profiling come to mind. Our best hope for a saner politics in which both forms of unfairness are redressed is a language based upon common values and common harms. For example, California sags under the weight of its prison budgets due in part to a racially unfair and fiscally insane war on drugs. California spends more on prisons than it does on higher education, and its public schools, once the envy of the nation, now rank near last in performance and per-pupil spending.[3] Fortunately, the state is beginning to self-correct. Californians recently voted to raise taxes in order to invest $6 billion annually in education, and they approved a measure that moderated the state's infamous "three-strikes" law that had required life sentences even for nonviolent, three-time felons. These developments suggest the emerging promise of multiracial politics.

Once we get started on a sanity alliance and begin to build trust and relationships, we can begin to have more honest, refreshing discussions about how racialized structures damage the whole. A sanity alliance might identify public and private policies that violate our antidiscrimination values and harm the common good, including mass incarceration, the war on drugs, and predatory lending. Then this coalition of the willing should organize state and local movements to reform those policies. Washington, DC, is nearly impossible these days. A better place to start is with the numerous multiracial coalitions that are already working in scores of communities, often in a bipartisan manner.

Throughout American history, economic elites used racial categories and racism to drive a wedge between working-class whites and people of color they might ally with. In the colonial era, indentured servitude gave way to white freedom and black slavery so that white servants no longer had incentive to join blacks in revolt, as they did in Bacon's Rebellion. In the late nineteenth century, Jim Crow laws proliferated after a biracial farmers' alliance threatened to change unfair financial policies imposed by elites. And the GOP devised a cynical, race-coded Southern strategy that broke up the multiracial alliance that made the New Deal possible. Given this history and its current manifestations, intentional efforts are sorely needed to begin to rebuild trust among "we the people" and to recapture a sense of collective will to protect the common good.

Race-based affirmative action in a context of ascending diversity will continue to fuel white resentment and division and is unnecessary when place-based alternatives that track *actual* disadvantage are available. One suggestion would be to substitute "low-opportunity neighborhood" for race as a plus factor in the type of formulas that universities use in admissions decisions because race is too blunt an instrument and too costly politically. Then, blow up and redo university admissions practices to eliminate unfair structural barriers that limit access and undermine university mission.

When the values of whites and people of color converge, and real efforts are made to build alliances among them, transformative change ensues. The abolition of slavery, Reconstruction, the civil rights movement, and Obama's election are great moments in our nation's history. I think the country is ripe for another leap forward, but progressives have to bring about reconciliation to make it happen. Each social transformation has been followed by a period of backlash, and there is evidence that we are in such a period now. Explicit racism that shows up in cyberspace and tragedies that render names like Trayvon household words are a warning sign—a reminder that in America, on matters of race, there is always a fire next time. We, the people, have to get better at how we respond to it.

A Letter to My Sons

Dear Langston and Logan,

I have written a book that undermines the possibility that you will ever benefit from affirmative action. When you are much older, you may read it to understand what that is, or what it used to be. I have great confidence in you, and believe you will amaze yourself and the world. Other children will not have the opportunities you have been given, and that is why I have written this book and why I am writing this letter to you. I wish to arm you with knowledge about how to be successful and what you must do to make our country better.

As difficult and challenging as it can be to be a black male, there are great rewards for the brothers who work overtime at academics. Many institutions will fight over you. Most Americans want to see you succeed, if only so that they can feel better about themselves and the society we have. You have to decide whether you will enter the fray that is elite higher education. The rules of the game have changed for everyone. You cannot depend on your name, or your color, or your parents' connections, although they may get you a close look. You must depend on yourself and your lifelong project of cultivating what is unique and precious about you. You have to choose. Other students who want to enter a great college will decide that they will do whatever it takes. They will put in extra hours, take the difficult classes. Hopefully, they will be motivated by a love of learning.

As I write this you are six—and three-quarters, you would remind me. Your curiosity is boundless. Your willingness to work at things is growing. Your dad and I push you. Like all the parents around you, we inflict our hopes onto you and schedule your lives accordingly. But one day, all too soon, you will have to choose your path.

Life will not always be fair to you. There are no safe, guaranteed routes. Every road eventually bends and presents risk. The approach I urge you to take is to welcome new challenges with the wonder of an explorer and persevere, as Grandma Harriette always says. While you are doing all the things school requires of you, figure out what you love and devote extra time to that. Work at your passion daily and see where it takes you. By passion I mean the thing you wake up thinking about, go to sleep dreaming about. The thing that you cannot put down, even when it frustrates you, even when you have doubts about whether you will ever be good at it. Your passion is what you want to do every day, for hours. If you are obsessed with something and that fervor persists, it is probably what God put you on earth to do. It is the secret to life, figuring out what you would do for free and then carving out time, daily, to do it. If you labor at it for years, with luck one day you may get to earn a living doing what nurtures your soul. If not, continue to do it in your spare time, simply because it gives meaning to your life, and occasionally great joy.

Your time on earth is limited. Do not spend it acquiring things. Consuming is time away from doing what you were put here to do. Consuming and what you have are not important. What you contribute while here is. You must also be wary of consuming too much television, video, electronics, social media, or any gadget or technology that distracts you from what matters. No one ever achieved greatness in front of a TV. No video game can compare to reading a book, to actively using your brain to think, write, paint, make music, or invent something. I will not give you permission to play games that are designed to addict you, not with my money.

While you are pursuing your passions, recognize that some things are required of you that you won't enjoy, and just deal with it. Work and work and work some more until you get it. Ask for help early when you don't, and then go back to work. That is what Cashins do, I was told. And that is what Chamblisses and Clarks do. That is what African American strivers have done from the beginning in America. They toiled in the face of adversity and persevered. It is a legacy you should be proud of and that you must continue.

Grandpa did it. I hope you will remember him, and not only as the old man we visited at the nursing home. Before he was confined to a wheelchair, before his voice diminished to a whisper and words eluded him, he strode proudly in the world and spoke fiercely about the things he felt compelled to do. He told stories about himself and our ancestors. At Fisk, the college he and his parents went to, he would get up at four or five in the morning to study when no one was around. He also was expelled for having a party in his dorm room, but he recovered from that mistake and went on to graduate first in his class from Meharry Medical College. Grandpa learned the habits of success from his mother, my Grandma Grace, a school principal who raised both of her sons to be valedictorians.

Grandpa's habits became my habits. I remember a day of studying in the Heard Library at Vanderbilt when final exams were upon me. I logged at least a dozen hours. I didn't think I had it in me, but there I sat and persevered. As each hour passed, I found new wells of strength. It never occurred to me to do something else, to not try that hard. Like Grandpa, I carved out solitary time for mind-work. My goal, the goal I was taught to reach for, was an A in every class. It is the reaching, not the grade, that matters.

This is your legacy. Do not be afraid of it. Embrace it and know that you are capable of more than you ever thought possible if you put in the time. You are fortunate to attend schools that are utterly stimulating, with teachers that send you home each day with new concepts that excite you. I am learning from you and relearning things I forgot. Sometimes it is tough. I know nothing of Mandarin, and the pressures of homework have begun. As you get older, these burdens will multiply. Take challenges in increments. Work at a task for as long as you can concentrate well on it, then take a walk to refresh. Then go back to work for another period, refresh, and then go back for a third. Hopefully three intense sessions, focusing only on your work, will be enough on most days. In crunch times you will need to do more, much more.

You have watched your father do it, toiling for hours at the computer, researching and writing papers for his master's degree. Always he gets an A. Not because he is smart, but because he tries *very* hard. He already had two degrees, from college and law school. In middle age, even with a full-time job, he decided to go back to school for a third degree, because he wanted to do more in life and he wanted to explore a subject that interested him. That is what is required to grow and succeed. You have to exert yourself. Everything worth doing is hard, difficult, complicated. You should welcome failure. Sometimes it is the only route to success. I failed repeatedly in trying to sell versions of this book to publishers. After each rejection I kept writing and experimenting with my ideas, a process that became joyful when I decided to set my ego aside. Again, if something is easy you are not challenging yourself or honoring your legacy.

Being a black male is wonderful and perilous. You don't have the luxury of being casual about your life, or it may be ruined in an instant. At a party, when kids of all colors smoke marijuana or drink alcohol, you may be the only one who gets arrested and hauled off to jail if the police are called. That is a true story a friend shared with me about a party of kids from the Dalton School in New York City. Everybody was doing it. Only the black boy was arrested.

This is an old story in America. Your great-great-grandfather, Herschel V. Cashin, was ejected violently from a train in Alabama in the 1890s because he sat where he wanted to. It didn't matter that he was a lawyer dressed like the patrician that he was. In the 1950s an Alabama state trooper clubbed Grandpa, my father, over the head with his police stick. The trooper knocked Grandpa unconscious when he exited his fancy convertible, speaking too confidently in the trooper's estimation after a stop for speeding. A policeman stopped me for driving too fast on a dark road in Avondale Estates, Georgia. It was 1986. I was skinny then, and it was implausible that he could have perceived me as a threat. The officer made me get out of the car and stand spread-eagle against it while he frisked me.

I could share more depressing stories of family members and friends who were treated unfairly by the criminal justice system—an oxymoron in the minds of most African Americans. In our extended, multi-degreed family, I know of seven males who have endured skirmishes with law enforcement, ranging from false arrests to actual imprisonment. Some were innocent. Some were not. As black males, you are at greater risk of being detained, hassled, interrogated or prosecuted than non-blacks who engage in similar conduct. America has "zero tolerance" for your mistakes. On the school playground, a hug of a classmate can get you written up as a predator. That is another depressing, true tale shared with me by a mother of a black boy just as loving and spirited as you are.

I do worry that I cannot protect you from predatory policing, gun violence, or the fact that US society will never love you the way I do. You must prepare for the day when you cease being adorable in the eyes of strangers. Even before your first facial hairs emerge, you will notice that some people are afraid of you. Social scientists call it automaticity. One cannot live in America without absorbing negative concepts about African Americans. The people who live farthest away from us often have the most unrealistic views about us.

There are places called ghettoes. By now you may have heard that word. The most extreme myths about what it means to be black come from these neighborhoods where too many people are poor. There are gangs, boys who shoot each other, sometimes over nothing but a demand for respect. Their fights are not that different than the ones you have with each other. Always I tell you to stop it, that your brother is supposed to be your best friend, and that you are supposed to protect him, not hurt him. These boys in the 'hood are the ones America most fears, and that subconscious anxiety will get transferred to you when you are walking on the street as teenagers.

I am guilty of it too; most of us are. A taut black guy walks his bulldog along 11th Street as I am driving home. I pause at a stoplight, look at him, and without thinking push the button to lock the already locked door. The lock clicks and the man hears it. His eyes meet mine, accusingly. "You too, sister?" he conveys. I am horrified at my automatic response. Some people feel justified in their negative assumptions about black people. I actively resist these impulses when I notice them operating and try to assess people based on how they actually behave, not how they look. You must do the same. Do not assume anything about a person. Get to know them, and try not to waste energy judging others.

I am so proud that you already possess empathy. You notice a homeless man on the street and ask about his life, how he got there, how he eats. You told your father the other day that you wanted to give your money to people who don't have very much. Giving and caring about others is also your legacy.

Grandma Harriette's mother and father gave repeatedly. Hattie and John Francis Clark raised five children in Charleston, West Virginia. Four of them became doctors and the fifth a lawyer. Great-grandpa Clark earned degrees from the University of Chicago and Harvard and became a high school principal, the leading educator of Negro children in Charleston. Hattie was a brilliant girl who became a schoolteacher at age fifteen and bought her first piece of land at seventeen. Your great-grandparents were always investing and building. They built a post office and leased it to the government. They started a family corporation that a third generation of descendants is now steering. In the Depression, the Clark home was filled to bursting with relatives and friends who had lost everything. One family lived on the back porch. Hattie Clark would take them in. Weekly, the black professors at West Virginia State would come to Hattie, asking her to co-sign notes to save their homes. She would buy their homes back for them when she could. She even paid off the mortgage for a black church.

Mommy and Daddy were following Hattie's example when we invited your cousin to live with us and sponsored her through college. It is another tradition you must continue. Take care of your family. Lift up the ones who stumble. They will lift you when you fall. You are so lucky to have a brother to turn to who knows you better than anyone, perhaps better than you know yourself. God sent you here together. It is a magnificent gift to be cherished and held on to.

Find your allies, whatever color they may be, and don't worry about those who may be hardest to connect with. Don't see them as bad or unreachable. Empathize with them, and move on. A maître d' once asked whether you would become a rapper or a ball player. "Aiming kind of high, aren't we?" he said when I suggested doctor or lawyer for my genius children instead. After my anger dissipated, it occurred to me that the maître d' may have been struggling to take care of his children on what he earned working in that restaurant. He may have envied your youth, your fresh chance to make better choices than he did. You enjoy advantages that his children do not.

That is why I do not believe you need or deserve affirmative action. It is not enough that you are an African American male, that you will be profiled, that some people see you as an endangered species, that you may offer a "black" perspective, whatever that is, in the classroom. There are other black children who have a lot less than you do who need the fair shot at life your parents are providing to you. And the maître d's children may have white skin to protect them from profiling, but your parents will soon have six degrees between them. If you apply to college and are allowed to benefit merely from the fact that you are black, then the maître d's resentment will continue, and we will be no further along in trying to create a country where people support policies that help black and brown children who are not advantaged.

I would trade the benefit to you of affirmative action for a country that does not fear and demonize people who look like you. We have to begin to heal this country, to set it on a new course of fairness. If we accept the system as it is—affirmative action and sequestered advantages for a few—we have given up, I think, on the idea of America. I'm not ready to do that.

So I will make no excuses for you if you cannot get into a great program of higher education on your own terms. Like other fortunate kids, you have developed an enormous sense of entitlement that will help you get what you want from life. You will need that to feel confident wherever you go. But do not ever think you are better or more deserving than others. You are not. Take your privileges and gifts and use them for the good of others. My inheritance, passed to me from Grandpa, was to care about other people's children. You are required to as well.

Our country is divided now, but that is not inevitable, nor permanent. Your multiracial generation, the first one in American history in which no one group is a majority, will be better than mine and all others that came before you. You are already better on the playground. You choose your friends based upon what they like to do and what is in their hearts. You and millions of other youth are changing what it means to be American. There is no single standard of American-ness anymore, no entitled race to which all others are subordinated. The perennial conundrum that your generation must take up is how all the different strains of humanity in America can cohere as a nation. Most important, can fear of poor people of color be overcome? I hope that your generation will learn to include rather than be afraid of them. Let them be a part of larger society. There is no other way. Build neighborhoods, schools, and places of stable inclusion. Include all types of people so that everyone may prosper. Otherwise, only those who were lucky at the lottery of birth will advance.

I will not burden you with the obligation of leadership. Only you can decide whether that is for you. I will insist that you be part of the coalition that agitates for something better than the separate and unequal system we now have. Do not play king of the hill. It is an ugly game that is unworthy of you. Put on your armor, prove others wrong in their assumptions about you, find your multiracial army, and fight together for the country you deserve.

ACKNOWLEDGMENTS

I could not have written this book without the assistance and support of many people. James Beckman, thank you for inviting me to write a chapter for a volume you edited about affirmative action. It took me down an unexpected path, gave me an opportunity to explore my instincts about place and disadvantage in college admissions, and spurred me to delve more broadly into the subject of place and fairness.

Lani Guinier, thank you for your pioneering work in this field and for recommending me to Beacon Press years ago; that seed grew into a book contract. Will Myers, thank you for asking me to write a blurb for a Beacon book. As a result, we began a conversation about ideas I had for books, and I greatly appreciated your encouragement. Joanna Green, thank you for believing in my proposal and championing it. Thank you also for being a gentle editor. You made me feel good about the work, even when some of it needed to be scrapped. Thank you as well to everyone at Beacon who contributed to the production and marketing of *Place, Not Race*.

My dear cousin Dorothy Reed, thank you for reading the entire manuscript and helping me to understand the core idea. As always, your insights and suggestions were invaluable. You are my earth angel.

Thanks so much to friends and colleagues who read and commented on all or parts of the manuscript: Spencer Overton and Olati Johnson, who were very generous in offering detailed comments on multiple chapters, as well as Phil Tegeler, Paul Scully, Mike Seidman, and participants in the Georgetown Law Faculty Workshop, especially Paul Butler, Gerry Spann, Larry Solum, Emma Jordan, and Allegra McCleod. All of you contributed in very important ways that made the book better. Paul Butler, thanks for our ongoing conversation about book writing, for reading my other, not-yet-successful book proposals, and inspiring me to be brave on matters of race. Gerry Spann and Randall Kennedy, thanks for offering contrary viewpoints that I had to take seriously and for your unfailing support. Thanks to my colleague and dear friend Julie Cohen for emotional support and counsel as I wrote this book.

Thank you also to Randall Kennedy and Charles Ogletree for being great teachers and mentors, and for the help you each offered me in recent years with book publishing.

Thank you to those who shared their perspectives with me in interviews for this book, including Connie Jackson, Tony Marx, and Tom Parker. Other interviewees chose anonymity. I am most grateful that you allowed me to share your powerful stories.

Thank you to my students over the years in Race and American Law. Some of your stories and insights found their way into this book. I learned a lot from you about what does and doesn't work in discussing race and how, ultimately, to create a community of trust.

Thank you to my dean, Bill Treanor, and associate dean Greg Klass for providing me with financial and emotional support in writing this book.

Marco Crocetti, thank you for spending a summer as my research assistant on this project. Time and again you unearthed empirical evidence to support my argument and helped advance my thinking. Heartfelt thanks to Aleshadye Getachew and Boris Zhao, who provided research assistance on academic projects that preceded but greatly influenced the content of this book. Many thanks to Esther Cho of Georgetown's Edward Bennett Williams Law Library, and to research assistants Eleanor Erney, Jennifer Brown, Daniel Woodard, Shamus Durac, and Aleshadye Getachew for critical fact checking and editing support. Esther, you exceeded the call of duty, especially at the eleventh hour.

My assistant, Patrick Kane, was a great aide and ally. Patrick, I will forever be grateful for your technical prowess in restoring scores of research files that I managed to delete. Thanks also to Angie Villarreal and the entire faculty support staff at Georgetown for your cheerful assistance.

Thanks, as always, to Peter Osnos and Esther Newberg for launching me as an author.

Thanks to my author girlfriends Dolen Perkins-Valdez, Natalie Hopkinson, Michele Norris, and Gwen Ifill, who have helped me with failed and successful attempts to place books and other pieces. You all inspire me. Thanks to Marita Golden, Natalie Hopkinson, Darlene Taylor, and all the women writers of color who lunch quarterly and talk writing. Your ideas for titles for this book were tantalizing, and your emotional support from beginning to end was a blessing. Thanks to the other girlfriends who read my work or encouraged me to keep plugging at it: Helen Howell, Crystal Nix-Hines, Lisa Davis, Cheryl Cooper, and Kumiki Gibson.

Finally, thank you to my family for enduring another book. My mother-in-law, Dr. Harriette Clark, and my stepmom, Dr. Louise White Cashin, encouraged me to persevere. My niece, Jasmine Cashin, did a great deal of babysitting. And my husband and children were kind to give me the time and space to write. Marque, Logan, and Langston, thank you for being my Misters Wonderful. I could not have done this without your love, support, and patience.

Several of the ideas in this book began with essays or articles I wrote for scholarly journals or presented for academic symposia or lectures. Hence, portions of the manuscript are adapted from parts of the following previously published works: "Place, Not Race: Affirmative Action and the Geography of Opportunity," in *Controversies in Affirmative Action*, ed. James Beckman (Westport, CT: ABC-CLIO/Praeger, 2014); "Shall We Overcome? 'Post-Racialism' and Inclusion in the 21st Century," *Alabama Civil Rights and Civil Liberties Law Review* 1 (2011): 31–47; "To Be Muslim or 'Muslim-Looking' in America: A Comparative Exploration of Racial and Religious Prejudice in the 21st Century," *Duke Forum for Law and Social Change* 2 (2010): 125–39; "Democracy, Race, and Multiculturalism in the Twenty-First Century: Will the Voting Rights Act Ever be Obsolete?" *Washington University Journal of Law and Policy* 22 (2006): 71–105; "Shall We Overcome? Transcending Race, Class, and Ideology Through Interest Convergence," *St. John's Law Review* 79 (2005): 253–91; and "The Civil Rights Act of 1964 and Coalition Politics," *St. Louis University Law Journal* 49 (2005): 1029–46.

NOTES

INTRODUCTION

1. C. Brett Lockhard and Michael Wolf, "Employment Outlook 2010–2020: Occupational Employment Projections to 2020," *Monthly Labor Review* 84 (January 2012): 106, table 6, which identifies "[j]ob openings due to growth and replacement needs, 2010–2020."

2. Charles Tilly, "How to Hoard Opportunities," in *Durable Inequality* (Berkeley: University of California Press, 1998), 147–69.

3. "Abigail Fisher v. University of Texas at Austin," YouTube video, posted by "FairRepresentation," September 4, 2012, http://www.youtube.com/watch?v=sXSpx9PZZj4.

4. Brief for Respondents University of Texas at Austin at 16, Fisher v. University of Texas at Austin, 132 S. Ct. 1536 (2012), no. 11–345.

5. Okla. Const. art. 2, § 36.

6. Rice University Office of Institutional Research, *Students and Scholars: Race and Ethnicity,* http://oir.rice.edu/Factbook/Students/Enrollment/Race_and_Ethnicity.

7. Sophia Hollander, "At Dalton, a Push for Change," *Wall Street Journal,* August 11, 2011, online.wsj.com/article/SB10001424053111903918104576500653887399330.html.

8. Tom McNamee, "Who Really Benefits From Colleges' Affirmative Action?" *Chicago Sun Times,* July 19, 2004.

9. Rasmussen Reports, "55% Oppose Affirmative Action Policies for College Admissions," February 26, 2012, http://www.rasmussenreports.com/public_content/politics/general_politics/february_2012/55_oppose_affirmative_action_policies_for_college_admissions.

10. Quinnipiac University Polling Institute, "US Voters Disagree 3–1 With Sotomayor On Key Case, Quinnipiac University National Poll Finds; Most Say Abolish Affirmative Action," June 3, 2009, http://www.quinnipiac.edu/institutes-and-centers/polling-institute/national/release-detail?ReleaseID=1307.

11. Ibid.

12. Pew Research Center Religion and Public Life Project, "Muslims Widely Seen as Facing Discrimination," September 9, 2009, http://www.pewforum.org/2009/09/09/muslims-widely-seen-as-facing-discrimination.

13. Paul Taylor, "Race, Ethnicity and Campaign '08," Pew Research Center, January 17, 2008, http://www.pewresearch.org/2008/01/17/race-ethnicity-and -campaign-08.

14. In 2012, "51 percent of Americans express[ed] explicit anti-black attitudes, compared with 48 percent in a similar 2008 survey. When measured by an implicit racial attitudes test, the number of Americans with anti-black sentiments jumped to 56 percent, up from 49 percent during the last presidential election." Sonya Ross and Jennifer Agiesta, "AP Poll: Majority Harbor Prejudice Against Blacks," Associated Press, October 27, 2012, http://bigstory.ap.org/article/ap-poll-majority-harbor -prejudice-against-blacks.

15. See Jerry Kang, "Trojan Horses of Race," *Harvard Law Review* 118 (2005): 1489–1593, which presents an overview of social psychology literature on implicit bias.

16. Pew Research Center Social and Demographic Trends Project, "King's Dream Remains an Elusive Goal; Many Americans See Racial Disparities," August 22, 2013, http://www.pewsocialtrends.org/files/2013/08/final_full_report_racial _disparities.pdf.

17. Joe Nocera, "What Gun Lovers Think," *New York Times*, April 6, 2013, www.nytimes.com/2013/04/07/opinion/sunday/nocera-what-gun-lovers-think .html?pagewanted=all&_r=0.

18. "Most Black Students at Harvard Are from High-Income Families," *Journal of Blacks in Higher Education* 52 (Summer 2006): 13.

19. Lyndon B. Johnson, "To Fulfill These Rights" (speech, Washington, DC, June 4, 1965), LBJ Presidential Library, http://www.lbjlib.utexas.edu/johnson/ archives.hom/speeches.hom/650604.asp.

20. Martin Luther King Jr., "Justice Without Violence" (speech, Waltham, MA, April 4, 1957), King Center, http://www.thekingcenter.org/archive/document/ mlk-justice-without-violence.

21. Martin Luther King Jr., "Letter from Birmingham Jail," in *Why We Can't Wait* (New York: Harper & Row, 1964), 77–100.

22. Martin Luther King Jr., *A Testament of Hope: The Essential Writings and Speeches of Martin Luther King, Jr.* (New York: HarperCollins, 1990), 253.

23. Sam Dillon, "Study Finds High Rate of Imprisonment Among Dropouts," *New York Times*, October 9, 2009, www.nytimes.com/2009/10/09/education/ 09dropout.html?_r=0.

CHAPTER ONE
White Resentment, the Declining Use of Race, and Gridlock

1. Sara Grossman, "UC Berkeley College Republicans' 'Diversity Bake Sale' Elicits Cries of Racism," *Daily Californian,* September 23, 2011, http://www .dailycal.org/2011/09/23/uc-berkeley-college-republican-bake-sale-elicits-cries-of -racism.

2. Colleen Curry, Kevin Dolak, and Olivia Katrandjian, "UC Berkeley Bake Sale Ignites Protests, Debates," ABC News, September 27, 2011, http://abcnews .go.com/US/berkeley-bake-sale-sparks-rallies-debate-race/story?id=14613509.

3. "SB 185 Vetoed: Jerry Brown Vetoes Affirmative Action-Like Bill," *Huffing-ton Post*, October 9, 2011, http://huffingtonpost.com.

4. Adarand Constructors, Inc. v. Pena, 515 US 200, 239 (1995).

5. Parents Involved in Community Schools v. Seattle School Dist. No. 1, 551 US 701, 748 (2007).

6. Even in cases like *McCleskey v. Kemp*, when presented with clear evidence of racial disparities in death penalty sentencing in Georgia, the Court has been unwilling to find a violation of the equal protection clause (McClesky v. Kemp, 481 US 279 [1987]). Blindness to such racial realities would seem to be the opposite of what the radical Republicans who drafted the Fourteenth Amendment hoped for.

7. The left flank of the Court has a different vision of equal protection, one that would distinguish between Jim-Crow style *exclusion* and use of race to *include* through programs like affirmative action. Justice Ginsberg, for example, would apply strict scrutiny only to the former; Grutter v. Bollinger, 539 US 306, 344 (2003). Ginsberg certainly rejected legal formalism and the fictions of colorblindness when she noted in her dissent in *Fisher* that there was nothing race-neutral about the residential segregation that enabled the Texas Ten Percent Plan to produce some diversity (Fisher v. University of Texas at Austin, 133 S. Ct. 2411, 2433 [2013]).

8. Shelby County v. Holder, 570 US 2 (2013).

9. See the Project for Fair Representation (http://www.projectonfair representation.org), which has been described as a one-man operation headed by Edward Blum that receives donations from a handful of conservative donors. Blum specializes in recruiting plaintiffs to challenge racial classifications and matching them with lawyers his organization pays. Abigail Fisher, whom he recruited, is the daughter of an old friend. Joan Biskupic, "Special Report: Behind US Race Cases, a Little Known Recruiter," Reuters, December 4, 2012, www.reuters.com/article/2012/12/04/us-usa-court-casemaker idUSBRE8B30V220121204. Blum also recruited plaintiffs in the *Shelby County* case and has been involved in more than a dozen cases challenging racial classification. Joan Biskupic and Howard Goller, "Cases Edward Blum has taken to the US Supreme Court," Reuters, December 4, 2012, www.reuters.com/article/2012/12/04/us-usa-court casemaker-cases -idUSBRE8B311220121204.

10. William M. Chace, "Affirmative Inaction," *American Scholar* 2 / (Winter 2011), http://theamericanscholar.org/affirmative-inaction. See also Thomas J. Espenshade et al., "Admission Preferences for Minority Students, Athletes, and Legacies at Elite Universities," *Social Science Quarterly* 85, no. 5 (December 2004): 1422–46 , which finds that admissions advantages experienced by African Americans and Latinos in college admissions are decreasing over time and corresponding advantages awarded to athletes are increasing.

11. Washington Post-ABC News, "Public Opposes Affirmative Action, Supports Same Sex Marriage," June 12, 2013, http://www.washingtonpost.com/politics/public-opposes-affirmative-action-supports-same-sex-marriage/2013/06/11/1512e076-d2e8-11e2-a73e-826d299ff459_graphic.html. See also George Curry, "Affirmative Action Polls Show Deep Racial Gulf," *The Skanner*, June 24, 2013,

http://www.theskanner.com/article/Affirmative-Action-Polls-Show-Deep-Racial
-Gulf-2013-06-24.

12. Pew Research Center, "Millennials: Confident. Connected. Open to Change," February 24, 2010, http://www.pewsocialtrends.org/2010/02/24/millennials-confident-connected-open-to-change.

13. Sheryll Cashin, "Democracy, Race, and Multiculturalism in the Twenty-First Century: Will the Voting Rights Act Ever be Obsolete?" *Washington University Journal of Law and Policy* 22 (2006): 71–105.

14. CNN Election Center, "Races & Results: Exit Polls," December 10, 2012, http://www.cnn.com/election/2012/results/race/president.

15. These numbers are based upon national exit polls in 2008 and 2012. For the Pew Center analysis, see Pew Research Center for the People and the Press, *A Closer Look at the Parties in 2012*, August 23, 2012, http://www.people-press.org/2012/08/23/a-closer-look-at-the-parties-in-2012.

16. Ibid.

17. Ibid.

18. See "Blacks in Survey Say Race Relations No Better with Obama," CNN, July 20, 2009, http://www.cnn.com/2009/POLITICS/06/25/obama.poll/index.html?iref=allsearch.

19. See Pew Research Center, "A Year After Obama's Election: Blacks Upbeat about Black Progress, Prospects," January 12, 2010, http://pewsocialtrends.org/pubs/749/blacks-upbeat-about-black-progress-obama-election.

20. Ibid.; see box, "Has the Country Done Enough to Give Blacks Equal Rights with Whites?"

21. See Richard P. Eibach and Joyce Ehrlinger, "Keep Your Eyes on the Prize: Reference Points and Racial Differences in Assessing Progress Toward Equality," *Personality and Social Psychology Bulletin* 32 (2006): 66–77.

22. See Michael I. Norton and Samuel R. Sommers, "Whites See Racism as a Zero-Sum Game That They Are Now Losing," *Perspectives on Psychological Science* 6 (2011): 215, http://www.people.hbs.edu/mnorton/norton%20sommers.pdf.

23. See Ronald Brownstein, "Why the White Working Class Is Alienated, Pessimistic," *National Journal*, May 31, 2011. Brownstein notes that the country ceased being majority white and working class in 2004 and cites a national survey on economic opportunity released by the Pew Charitable Trusts' Economic Mobility Project.

24. Ibid.

25. See Rakesh Kochhar et al., *Wealth Gaps Rise to Record Highs between Whites, Blacks, Hispanics: Twenty-to-One*, Pew Research Center, July 26, 2011, http://www.pewsocialtrends.org/2011/07/26/wealth-gaps-rise-to-record-highs-between-whites-blacks-hispanics.

26. Camille L. Ryan and Julie Siebens, "Educational Attainment in the United States: 2009," US Census Bureau, February 2012, http://www.census.gov/prod/2012pubs/p20-566.pdf.

27. Hope Yen, "Exclusive: Signs of Declining Economic Security," Associated Press, July 28, 2013. This story cites new research by academics Mark Rank, Tom Hirschl, and John Iceland defining economic insecurity as joblessness, near-poverty, or reliance on welfare for at least part of one's life as a circumstance that four out of five US adults will endure by age sixty, and says such hardship is particularly on the rise for whites.

28. Rachel Godsil and Alexis McGill Johnson, "Resetting a Vision of Race for the 21st Century: Insights from the Mind Sciences," American Values Institute, August 13, 2013, 4, http://www.scribd.com/doc/163496747/Talking-About-Race-Memo.

29. This phenomenon was illustrated powerfully to me at a conference of law professors of color. Four African American law professors, myself included, were having a drink at the end of a long day, and the conversation turned from papers presented at the conference to lived realities. Everyone at the table was subsidizing relatives. One woman said that she and her husband regularly redistribute a third of their income to family members. Another stated that he helps about forty relatives and sets aside an amount annually to be distributed through a family foundation administered by his sister. In other contexts, I have swapped stories with upper-middle-class blacks who have relatives in varying stages of the criminal justice system. African Americans are more likely than non-blacks to perceive a racialized architecture of opportunity that negatively affects people of color because of these shared realities.

30. Lawrence Bobo et al., "Laissez Faire Racism: The Crystallization of a 'Kindler, Gentler' Anti-Black Ideology," in *Racial Attitudes in the 1990s: Continuity and Change*, ed. Steven A. Tuch and Jack K. Martin (Westport: Praeger, 1997), 15–44.

31. Pew Research Center, "A Year After Obama's Election," 92–94.

32. Cheryl R. Kaiser et al., "The Ironic Consequences of Obama's Election: Decreased Support for Social Justice," *Journal of Experimental Social Psychology* 45 (May 2009): 556, 558.

33. Sonya Ross and Jennifer Agiesta, "AP Poll: Majority Harbor Prejudice Against Blacks," Associated Press, October 27, 2012, http://bigstory.ap.org/article/ap-poll-majority-harbor-prejudice-against-blacks.

34. Ibid. Racial resentment was measured in the AP poll by a series of questions measuring each population's attitudes toward certain racial groups, word association with races (i.e., are they lazy, aggressive, etc.), each race's responsibility for their position and racial tension, and whether certain racial groups deserve their position in society. GfK, "Racial Attitudes Survey," Associated Press, October 29, 2012, http://surveys.ap.org/data%5CGfK%5CAP_Racial_Attitudes_Topline_09182012.pdf.

35. See Cashin, "Democracy, Race, and Multiculturalism in the Twenty-First Century," 80–84, which explains the politics of white supremacy in the states of the former confederacy, citing sources.

36. Despite protests to the contrary, there is some evidence to suggest that the Tea Party–led backlash against Obama had racial overtones. See David E.

Campbell and Robert D. Putnam, "Crashing the Tea Party," *New York Times*, August 16, 2011. The authors, as part of ongoing research into political attitudes, interviewed a representative sample of three thousand Americans in 2006, and returned to interview many of the same people again in 2011 after they had become members of the newly formed Tea Party. They found that Tea Party members were overwhelmingly socially conservative white Republicans. Even compared to other white Republicans, they had registered a low regard for immigrants and blacks long before Barack Obama was president, and they still held those views.

37. See Antoine J. Banks and Nicholas A. Valentino, "Emotional Substrates of White Racial Attitudes," *American Journal of Political Science* 56 (April 2012): 286–97.

38. Ibid.

39. Jonathan Weiler, "Racial Resentment, Authoritarianism and Health Care Reform," *Huffington Post*, September 2, 2009, http://www.huffingtonpost.com/jonathan-weiler/racial-resentment-authori_b_274475.html, citing Marc J. Hetherington and Jonathan D. Weiler, *Authoritarianism and Polarization in American Politics* (New York: Cambridge University Press, 2009).

40. Ibid.

41. Ibid. Party attachments became more polarized by racial attitudes after Obama became the titular head of the Democratic Party. Tesler and Sears found that voters high on a racial-resentment scale intensified their partisanship within the Republican Party by one notch on a seven-point scale that ranged from strong Democrat to Independent to strong Republican. Michael Tesler and David O. Sears, *Obama's Race: The 2008 Edition and the Dream of a Post-Racial America* (Chicago: University of Chicago Press, 2010).

42. Keesha Gaskins and Sundeep Iyer, *The Challenge of Obtaining Voter Identification*, Brennan Center for Justice, July 18, 2012, http://www.brennancenter.org/publication/challenge-obtaining-voter-identification.

43. "Voting Laws Roundup 2013," Brennan Center for Justice, August 15, 2013, http://www.brennancenter.org/analysis/election-2013-voting-laws-roundup.

44. Banks and Valentino, "Emotional Substrates of White Racial Attitudes," 296.

45. See J. Gainous, "The New 'New Racism' Thesis: Limited Government Values and Race-Conscious Policy Attitudes," *Journal of Black Studies* 43 (2012): 251–73.

46. Ibid. See also Tesler and Sears, *Obama's Race*.

47. See Dan Kahan, "Fixing the Communications Failure," *Nature* 463 (2010): 296–97; Dan Kahan et al., "Cultural Cognition of Scientific Consensus," *Journal of Risk Research* 14 (2010): 147–74. Kahan et al. offer a cultural cognition thesis, suggesting that people form perceptions that reflect and reinforce their worldview. They tested this thesis against issues for which there was scientific consensus—global warming, gun control, and nuclear power. Their data confirmed that peoples' perceptions are based on their values. Those with hierarchical and individual values thought that the scientists did not agree on these issues. People

with egalitarian and communitarian values were more likely to say there was a scientific consensus.

48. See David K. Sherman and Geoffrey L. Cohen, "The Psychology of Self-Defense: Self-Affirmation Theory," *Advances in Experimental Social Psychology* 38 (2006): 212. This is consistent with Eduardo Bonilla-Silva's claim that many whites harbor one of four "colorblind" frames of reference: that racial disparities do not exist, that such disparities are due to culture, that disparities are natural, or that race consciousness is unfair. See Eduardo Bonilla-Silva, *Racism Without Racists: Color-Blind Racism and the Persistence of Racial Inequality in the United States* (Lanham, MD: Rowman & Littlefield, 2003), 26.

49. "Big Racial Divide Over Zimmerman Verdict: Whites Say Too Much Focus on Race, Blacks Disagree," Pew Research Center, July 22, 2013, http://www .people-press.org/2013/07/22/big-racial-divide-over-zimmerman-verdict.

50. Gary Langer, "Vast Racial Gap on Trayvon Martin Case Marks a Challenging Conversation," ABC News, July 22, 2013, http://abcnews.go.com/blogs/ politics/2013/07/vast-racial-gap-on-trayvon-martin-case-marks-a-challenging -conversation.

51. Earl Black and Merle Black, *The Rise of Southern Republicans* (Cambridge, MA: Harvard University Press, 2002), 246–47.

52. Ibid., 380–86.

53. Ibid., 246–47.

54. See, generally, Keesha Gaskins, "200 Years of the Gerrymander," Brennan Center for Justice, March 26, 2012, http://www.brennancenter.org/blog/200-years -gerrymander; Matthew Frankel, "US Congress: Gerrymandering Is the Problem," Brookings Institution, June 15, 2010, http://www.brookings.edu/blogs/up-front/ posts/2010/06/15-gerrymandering-frankel; Jowei Chen, "The Effect of Electoral Geography on Competitive Elections and Partisan Gerrymandering," Jowei Chen's website, November 12, 2012, http://www-personal.umich.edu/~jowei/Chen _Wisconsin_14Sept2012.pdf.

55. Charlie Cook, "The GOP Keeps Getting Whiter," *National Journal*, March 14, 2013. Most recently, the Census Bureau predicted that non-Hispanic whites would become a minority by 2043 (US Census Bureau, "US Census Bureau Projections Show a Slower Growing, Older, More Diverse Nation a Half Century from Now," December 12, 2012, www.census.gov/newsroom/releases/archives/population/ cb12-243.html).

56. See, generally, *Partisan Polarization Surges in Bush, Obama Years; Trends in American Values: 1987–2012*, Pew Research Center, June 4, 2012, http://www .people-press.org/files/legacy-pdf/06-04-12ValuesRelease.pdf.

57. See, generally, Bill Bishop and Robert Cushing, *The Big Sort: Why the Clustering of Like-Minded America Is Tearing Us Apart* (New York: Houghton Mifflin, 2008).

58. Jennifer L. Hochschild, "Affirmative Action as Culture War," in *The Cultural Territories of Race: Black and White Boundaries*, ed. Michèle Lamont (Chicago: University of Chicago Press and Russell Sage Foundation, 1999), 343–68.

59. Ibid.

60. Richard Fry, *Hispanic College Enrollment Spikes, Narrowing Gaps with Other Groups*, Pew Research Center, August 25, 2011, http://www.pewhispanic.org/2011/08/25/hispanic-college-enrollment-spikes-narrowing-gaps-with-other-groups.

61. Julia Preston, "National Push by a Local Immigration Activist: No G.O.P. Retreat," *New York Times*, August 6, 2013.

62. See John B. Judis and Ruy Teixeira, *The Emerging Democratic Majority* (New York: Simon and Shuster, 2002), 6, 74–76.

63. Banks and Valentino, "Emotional Substrates of White Racial Attitudes," 296.

CHAPTER TWO
Place Matters

1. Between 1968 and 1988, integration increased steadily, such that the percentage of black children in the South attending integrated schools rose from near zero when *Brown* was decided to 43.5 percent in 1988. Since the early 1990s, schools have resegregated rapidly as the Supreme Court relaxed standards for ending school desegregation orders. See Sheryll Cashin, *The Failures of Integration: How Race and Class Are Undermining the American Dream* (New York: PublicAffairs, 2004), 211–18.

2. Gary Orfield, John Kucsera, and Genevieve Siegel-Hawley, *E Pluribus . . . Separation: Deepening Double Segregation for More Students*, Civil Rights Project, September 2012, 6–11, http://civilrightsproject.ucla.edu/research/k-12-education/integration-and-diversity/mlk-national/e-pluribus...separation-deepening-double-segregation-for-more-students. See also Myron Orfield and Thomas Luce, "America's Racially Diverse Suburbs: Opportunities and Challenges," Institute on Metropolitan Opportunity, July 20, 2012, 39, www.law.umn.edu/uploads/5f/ob/5f0b8b86d389c4416a08bb29a3614ed2/Diverse_Suburbs_FINAL.pdf. Orfield and Luce note that "forty years of history and data demonstrate that integrated neighborhoods in regions with large-scale, metro-wide school-integration plans were much more stable than in metropolitan areas without such plans."

3. Howard A. White, *The Freedmen's Bureau in Louisiana* (Baton Rouge: Louisiana State University Press, 1970), 193; Louis R. Harlan, "Desegregation in New Orleans Public Schools During Reconstruction," *American Historical Review* 67, no. 3 (April 1962): 663–75.

4. john a. powell, "The Tensions Between Integration and School Reform," *Hastings Constitutional Law Quarterly* 28 (2001): 55.

5. Brown v. Board of Education of Topeka, 347 US 483 (1954) at 493.

6. powell, "Tensions," 658; see also Michelle Adams, "Radical Integration," *California Law Review* 94 (2006): 261, concerning housing integration.

7. Implementation of *Brown* in the 1970s accomplished salutary integration in many places until it was shut down by the Supreme Court. See Erwin Chemerinsky, "The Segregation and Resegregation of American Public Education: The Court's Role," *North Carolina Law Review* 81 (2003): 1597.

8. Parents Involved in Cmty. Sch. v. Seattle Sch. Dist. No. 1, 551 US 701 (2007). For guidance from the Obama administration on how school integration can be pursued under the *Parents Involved* standards, see US Department of Education, Civil Rights Division, and the US Department of Education, Office for Civil Rights, "Guidance On The Voluntary Use Of Race To Achieve Diversity And Avoid Racial Isolation In Elementary And Secondary Schools," www2.ed.gov/about/offices/list/ocr/docs/guidance-cse-201111.pdf.

9. Henceforth, when I use the term *white*, I mean non-Hispanic white. I will use Hispanic or Latino to connote persons of that ethnicity.

10. John R. Logan, *Separate and Unequal: The Neighborhood Gap for Blacks, Hispanics, and Asians in Metropolitan America*, US2010 Project, 2010, 2–3, www.s4.brown.edu/us2010/Data/Report/report0727.pdf.

11. John R. Logan and Brian J. Stults, *The Persistence of Segregation in the Metropolis: New Findings from the 2010 Census*, US2010 Project, March 24, 2011, 6, www.s4.brown.edu/us2010/Data/Report/report2.pdf.

12. Ibid., 5.

13. Logan, *Separate and Unequal*, 5.

14. Logan and Stults, *The Persistence of Segregation*.

15. Ibid., 9.

16. The dissimilarity index measures the proportion of minority members who would have to move to be evenly distributed across a given region. After increasing dramatically during the first half of the twentieth century, especially in Northern cities, black/white racial segregation began to slowly decline in the 1960s or 1970s. See Douglas Massey and Nancy Denton, *American Apartheid: Segregation and the Making of the Underclass* (Cambridge, MA: Harvard University Press, 1993). Black/white dissimilarity has continued to decline slowly through the 2000s. According to the 2010 census, the black/white dissimilarity index nationally was 59.1. Logan and Stults, *The Persistence of Segregation*, 3, 23.

17. Logan and Stults, *The Persistence of Segregation*.

18. Edward Glaeser and Jacob Vigdor, "The End of the Segregated Century: Racial Separation in America's Neighborhood, 1890–2010," Manhattan Institute, January 2012, http://www.manhattan-institute.org/html/cr_66.htm.

19. Elizabeth Kneebone et al., "The Re-Emergence of Concentrated Poverty: Metropolitan Trends in the 2000s," Brookings Institution, November 2011, www.brookings.edu/research/papers/2011/11/03-poverty-kneebone-nadeau-berube. "Concentrated poverty" is a term favored by demographers for neighborhoods where at least 40 percent of the residents are poor. After proliferating in the 1970s and 1980s, high-poverty neighborhoods declined by nearly 30 percent in the prosperous 1990s and then resurged in the economic dislocations of the 2000s, as did the size of the population living in there. About 2,800 census tracts or neighborhoods fall into this category, and they are home to over 8 million people (ibid., 5, and table 1).

20. Over two-thirds of children living in ghetto neighborhoods in the early 1970s still live in a similar neighborhood today. Patrick Sharkey, *Stuck in Place:*

Urban Neighborhoods and the End of Progress Toward Racial Equality (Chicago: University of Chicago Press, 2013).

21. For an overview of the current and historical policy choices that promote segregation, see Cashin, *Failures of Integration*, 83–126. See also Jonathan T. Roth-well and Douglas S. Massey, "Density Zoning and Class Segregation in US Metro-politan Areas," 2008, http://papers.ssrn.com/sol3/papers.cfm?abstract_id=1322128.

22. john a. powell, "Opportunity-Based Housing," *Journal of Affordable Housing & Community Development Law* (2002): 195–96; Patrick Sharkey, *Neighborhoods and the Black-White Mobility Gap*, Economic Mobility Project, Pew Charitable Trust, 2009, http://www.pewtrusts.org/uploadedFiles/wwwpewtrustsorg/Reports/Economic_Mobility/PEW_SHARKEY_v12.pdf.

23. Robert J. Sampson et al., "Durable Effects of Concentrated Disadvantage on Verbal Ability among African American Children," *Proceedings of the National Academy of Sciences of the United States of America* (January 22, 2008): 845–52; Geoffrey T. Wodtke et al., "Neighborhood Effects in Temporal Perspective: The Impact of Long-Term Exposure to Concentrated Disadvantage on High School Graduation," *American Sociological Review* 76 (2011): 713.

24. US Census Bureau, "Income, Poverty, and Health Insurance Coverage in the United States: 2010," US Census Bureau, September 2011, 7, www.census.gov/prod/2011pubs/p60–239.pdf. The Kirwan Institute at Ohio State has per-formed opportunity mapping analyses in ten states and localities. In Massachu-setts, 90 percent of blacks and Latinos live in areas of low opportunity, compared to only 31 percent of whites. Jason Reece et al., *People, Place and Opportunity*, (Kirwan Institute, 2009), 2–3, www.kirwaninstitute.osu.edu/reports/2009/11_2009_CTOppMapping_FullReport.pdf. In King County, Washington, 75 percent of the black population was isolated in low and very low opportunity places (ibid., 5).

25. Rachel Godsil and Alexis McGill Johnson, "Resetting a Vision of Race for the 21st Century: Insights from the Mind Sciences," American Values Institute, August 13, 2013, http://www.scribd.com/doc/163496747/Talking-About-Race-Memo. Godsil and McGill Johnson note, "White people—for whom discussions of race are often guilt inducing—often shut down entirely and cease listening." See also Alexis McGill Johnson and Rachel D. Godsil, "Transforming Perception: Black Men and Boys," American Values Institute, March 5, 2013, 12–13, www.perception.org/wordpress/wp-content/uploads/2013/03/BMR2_EXEC_HI_RES.pdf, which cites social science studies showing white anxiety about being perceived racist and attendant defensiveness and diminished cognitive function.

26. powell, "Oppotunity-Based Housing."

27. Kendra Bischoff and Sean F. Reardon, "Residential Segregation by Income, 1970–2009," US2010 Project, October 16, 2013, http://www.s4.brown.edu/us2010/Data/Report/report10162013.pdf; Sean F. Reardon and Kendra Bischoff, "Income Inequality and Income Segregation," *American Journal of Sociology*, 116 (2011): 1115–25. Another recent study based on the nation's thirty largest metro areas showed a similar rise in residential segregation by income. See Sean F. Reardon and

Kendra Bischoff, "Growth in the Residential Segregation of Families by Income, 1970–2009," US2010 Project, 2011, http://www.s4.brown.edu/us2010/Data/Report/report111111.pdf.

28. Elizabeth Kneebone and Alan Berube, *Confronting Suburban Poverty in America* (Washington: Brookings Institution Press, 2013), 18; Kneebone et al., "The Re-Emergence of Concentrated Poverty."

29. Kneebone and Berube, *Confronting Suburban Poverty*, 13, 16.

30. Ibid, 51. For a searing portrait of the social decay and loss of civic capital that occurred with deindustrialization in a formerly middle-class town, see Robert Putnam, "Crumbling American Dreams," *New York Times,* August 3, 2013, opinionator.blogs.nytimes.com/2013/08/03/crumbling-american-dreams/?_r=0, describing his hometown, Port Clinton, Ohio.

31. Richard Florida, "Mobility Is Prevented by a Class and Skill Divide," *New York Times*, July 24, 2013, www.nytimes.com/roomfordebate/2013/07/23/should-cities-specialize/a-class-and-skill-divide-prevents-mobility.

32. Ibid.

33. Monica Potts, "The Weeklies," *American Prospect*, March 26, 2013, http://prospect.org/article/weeklies.

34. Mike Tolson, "Income Segregation Fills the Suburbs," *Houston Chronicle*, October 13, 2012, www.chron.com/news/houston-texas/article/Income-segregation-fills-the-suburbs-3946236.php.

35. Reardon and Bischoff, "Income Inequality," 1139.

36. Douglas S. Massey, *Categorically Unequal: The American Stratification System* (New York: Russell Sage Foundation, 2007), 19.

37. For a detailed explanation of how affluent jurisdictions received a disproportionate share of infrastructure investments and how the fracturing of metro regions into scores, hundreds, and sometimes thousands of local jurisdictions pursuing parochial self-interest creates a zero-sum state politics in which middle- and upper-class suburbs fare best, see Cashin, *Failures of Integration*, 266–75.

38. Massey, *Categorically Unequal*.

39. Income mobility was also higher in places with stronger public schools, more civic engagement, and more two-parent families. Race was not a major factor in explaining these differences. Raj Chetty et al., "Summary of Project Findings," Equality of Opportunity Project, July 2013, http://obs.rc.fas.harvard.edu/chetty/website/IGE/Executive%20Summary.pdf.

40. Chad Stone et al., "A Guide to Statistics on Historical Trends in Income Inequality," Center on Budget and Policy Priorities, September 11, 2013, http://www.cbpp.org/cms/?fa=view&id=3629.

41. The Gini coefficient measures the level of inequality within a country. A higher Gini coefficient means fewer people hold a larger portion of a country's wealth. The Gini coefficient for household wealth in the United States has risen from 38.6 in 1968 to as high as 46.9 in 2010. However, New York University economist Edward Wolff estimated the Gini coefficient in 2009 to be 86.5, which represents a dramatically higher level of inequality. See "US Income Distribution: Just

How Unequal?" Inequality.org, February 14, 2012, http://www.inequality.org/unequal-americas-income-distribution.

42. Lawrence Mishel and Natalie Sabadish, "CEO Pay in 2012 Was Extraordinarily High Relative to Typical Workers and Other High Earners," Economic Policy Institute, June 26, 2013, 2, http://www.epi.org/publication/ceo-pay-2012-extraordinarily-high.

43. Jacob S. Rugh and Douglas S. Massey, "Racial Segregation and the American Foreclosure Crisis," *American Sociological Review* 75, no. 5 (October 2010): 629, www.asanet.org/images/journals/docs/pdf/asr/Oct10ASRFeature.pdf. In this article, Douglass Massey and PhD candidate Jacob Rugh use data from the one hundred largest US metropolitan areas to confirm a causal relationship between black segregation and the number and rate of foreclosures in a given metropolitan area. In other words, pervasive residential segregation (itself the result of decades of discriminatory practices) created ideal conditions for predatory lending. Segregated black and Latino neighborhoods were an easy target for risky subprime loans that were in great demand for use in mortgage-backed securities to be sold to secondary markets. The study authors conclude that Hispanic and black racial segregation was a key contributing cause of the foreclosure crisis. This racialized targeting of black and Latino neighborhoods and borrowers for risky subprime loans to satisfy corporate greed did great harm, not just to its immediate victims but also to anyone affected by the collapse of the mortgage market and the subsequent financial crisis.

44. US Census Bureau, "Educational Attainment in the United States: 2009," August 8, 2013, www.census.gov/prod/2012pubs/p20-566.pdf. The seventeen counties where more than half of the population twenty-five years and older held at least a bachelor's degree included suburban counties in the Northeast and elsewhere, counties with large universities or research facilities, and resort counties in the Western states.

45. Thurston Domina, "Brain Drain and Brain Gain: Rising Educational Segregation in the United States, 1940–2000," *City and Community* 5, no. 4 (December 2006): 394.

46. Ibid.; Douglas S. Massey et al., "The Changing Bases of Segregation in the United States," *Annals of the American Academy of Political and Social Science* 626 (November 2009): 74–90.

47. Domina, "Brain Drain," table 4.

48. This statement was made during a private discussion about affirmative action at a 2013 meeting of law professors who teach race and American law.

49. Janet M. Ruane and Karen A. Cerulo, *Second Thoughts: Sociology Challenges Conventional Wisdom* (Thousand Oaks, CA: Pine Forge Press, 2012), 130.

50. Orfield et al., *E Pluribus*, 7.

51. Nancy McArdle et al., "Segregation and Exposure to High-Poverty Schools in Large Metropolitan Areas: 2008–09," diversitydata.org, September 2010, http://diversitydata.sph.harvard.edu/Publications/school_segregation_report.pdf.

52. Orfield et al., *E Pluribus*, 2.

53. F. Cadelle Hemphill et al., "Achievement Gaps: How Hispanic and White Students in Public Schools Perform in Mathematics and Reading on the National Assessment of Education Progress," National Center for Education Statistics, June 2011, nces.ed.gov/nationsreportcard/pdf/studies/2011459.pdf.

54. James S. Coleman, "Equality of Educational Opportunity," *Equity and Excellence in Education* 6, no. 5 (1968); Cashin, *Failures of Integration*, 83–126; Richard D. Kahlenberg, *All Together Now: Creating Middle-Class Schools through Public School Choice* (Washington, DC: Brookings Institution Press, 2001).

55. Aron Trombka et al., "Strengthening the Moderately Priced Dwelling Unit Program: A 30 Year Review," Montgomery County Council, February 2004, http://www6.montgomerycountymd.gov/content/council/pdf/archive/pr/2004/0205mpdu.pdf.

56. Heather Schwartz, *Housing Policy Is School Policy: Economically Integrative Housing Promotes Academic Success in Montgomery County, Maryland* (New York: Century Foundation, 2010), 33–34.

57. Low-poverty schools are twenty-two times as likely to be high performing as high-poverty schools (Douglas N. Harris, *Ending the Blame Game on Educational Inequity: A Study of 'High Flying' Schools and NCLB* [Tempe, AZ: Education Policy Studies Laboratory, March 2006], 22). Low-income students in high-poverty schools are two years behind low-income students in more affluent schools (US Department of Education, Institute of Education Sciences, *The Nation's Report Card, Mathematics 2007: National Assessment of Educational Progress at Grades 4 and 8*, September 1997, 8, http://nces.cd.gov/nationsreportcard/pdf/main1007/2007494.pdf).

58. Valerie Strauss, "New Analysis Blasts Obama's School Turnaround Policy—and Tells How to Fix It," *Washington Post*, July 28, 2010, http://voices.washingtonpost.com/answer-sheet/education-secretary-duncan/analysis-blasts-obamas-school-turnaround-policy.html; Lawyers Committee for Civil Rights under Law, et al., "Framework for Providing All Students an Opportunity to Learn through Reauthorization of the Elementary and Secondary Education Act," July 2010, http://www.lawyerscommittee.org/admin/site/documents/files/Framework-for-Providing-All-Students-an-Opportunity-to-Learn.pdf.

59. US Department of Education, *Title I—Improving the Academic Achievement of the Disadvantaged*, 2004, www.ed.gov/policy/elsec/leg/csea02/pg1.html.

60. Richard Kahlenberg, *Turnaround Schools That Work: Moving Beyond Separate but Equal* (Washington, DC: Century Foundation, November 11, 2009) http://tcf.org/work/education/detail/turnaround-schools-that-work-moving-beyond-separate-but-equal.

61. In 2012, the Harlem Children Zone academies benefited from unrestricted revenue of $125,808,866 and had total expenses of $90,709,493 ("Consolidated Financial Statements Together with Report of Independent Certified Public Accountants," Harlem Children's Zone, June 30, 2012, http://hcz.org/images/stories/pdfs/HCZ%20Audited%20Financial%20Statements_2012.pdf).

62. Kahlenberg, *Turnaround Schools*, 15–16.

63. Logan, *Separate and Unequal*, 2.

64. Andreas Schleicher, *Preparing Teachers and Developing School Leaders for the 21st Century*, Organisation for Economic Co-Operation and Development, www.oecd.org/site/eduistp2012/49850576.pdf. This report notes that the US K-12 system reinforces the disadvantages of segregation, while other OECD countries mitigate these disadvantages by devoting more resources to low-opportunity schools, putting the most talented teachers there, and financing education at the state rather than the local level.

65. For a detailed overview of the social science and arguments regarding public education see Cashin, *Failures of Integration*, 202–36.

66. John U. Ogbu et al., *Minority Status, Oppositional Culture, and Schooling* (New York: Routledge, 2008).

67. I raised the question with students in my Race and American Law class at Georgetown Law in the spring of 2013, and three black males promptly testified to their personal experience with the phenomenon. One had experienced it in 2010 as a grade-school teacher placed by Teach for America in a high-poverty, nearly all-black elementary school. He had to interrupt his teaching in his first week of class to disabuse his pupils of the notion that working hard was acting white.

68. See Ta-Nehisi Coates, "Beyond the Code of the Streets," *New York Times*, May 4, 2013; William Julius Wilson, "More Than Just Race: Being Black and Poor in the Inner City," *Poverty & Race* (May/June 2009).

69. See Jerry Kang et al., "Implicit Bias in the Courtroom," *UCLA Law Review* 59, no. 5 (March 20, 2012), www.uclalawreview.org/?p=3576; Justin D. Levinson et al., "Guilty by Implicit Racial Bias: The Guilty/Not Guilty Implicit Association Test," *Ohio State Journal of Criminal Law* 8 (2010–2011): 87; Adam Benforado, "Quick on the Draw: Implicit Bias and the Second Amendment," *Oregon Law Review* 89, no. 1 (2010): 1; Elizabeth Anderson, "Why Racial Integration Remains an Imperative," *Poverty and Race* 20, no. 4 (July/August 2011): 1–2, www .prrac.org/newsletters/julaug2011.pdf (noting that segregation creates worldviews that are impervious to counterevidence and that those who have little contact with an out-group tend to view extreme and deviant behaviors of some members, such as violent crimes, as representative of the out-group).

70. One successful model developed by an organization called Blue Engine is a team-teaching approach that arms a teacher with four full-time teaching assistants to create, at great cost, a student teacher ratio of 6:1. Low-income students achieved significant gains when they had not only an excellent teacher but also a teacher assistant at their elbow that would monitor, coach, and correct mistakes as they arose. David Bornstein, "A Team Approach to Get Students College Ready," *New York Times*, May 15, 2013, http://opinionator.blogs.nytimes.com/2013/05/15/a-team-approach-to -get-students-college-ready/?_r=0.

71. Erica Frankenberg et al., *Choice without Equality: Charter School Segregation and the Need for Civil Rights Standards,* UCLA Civil Rights Project, January 2010, http://civilrightsproject.ucla.edu/research/k-12-education/integration -and-diversity/choice-without-equity-2009-report; Julie Mead and Preston Green,

Chartering Equity: Using Charter School Legislation and Policy to Advance Equal Educational Opportunity, National Education Policy Center, February 21, 2012, http://nepc.colorado.edu/publication/chartering-equity.

72. Yu-Ying is far ahead of district averages and increasing in performance annually. In 2012, 63 percent of its students were proficient in math and 72 percent in reading, not as high as affluent west-of-the-park schools but good enough for this author.

73. Vanessa De La Torre, "Hartford Journalism and Media Academy Set to Become a Magnet School," *Hartford (CT) Courant,* April 9, 2013, http://articles.courant.com/2013–04–09/community/hc-hartford-journalism-academy-0409–20130408_1_magnet-school-regional-school-choice-office-sheff. Eighty-one percent of blacks and 79 percent of Hispanics in Connecticut live in low-opportunity neighborhoods ("Opportunity in Connecticut," Connecticut Association for Human Services, February 2012, www.cahs.org/pdf/OpportunityInCT.pdf). Hartford students who attend magnet or suburban schools significantly outperform those who attend neighborhood schools (Connecticut State Department of Education, "CMT/CAPT Results for Hartford Resident Students," Connecticut State Department of Education, September 3, 2013, http://s3.amazonaws.com/s3.documentcloud.org/documents/786243/hartford-student-outcomes-based-on-school-type.pdf).

74. Richard D. Kahlenberg, "From All Walks of Life," *American Educator* (Winter 2012–2013), www.aft.org/pdfs/americaneducator/winter1213/Kahlenberg.pdf.

75. Parents Involved in Community Schools v. Seattle School District No. 1, 551 US 701, 778 (2006).

76. For example, Chicago combats hundreds of gangs that flourish in just 3 percent of its land base—mostly neighborhoods south and west of its downtown. In the first six months of 2013 it spent over $30 million in police overtime and over $40 million in targeted youth development, while employing a litany of other costly strategies to reduce its tragic murder rate (Monica Davey, "Chicago Tactics Put Major Dent in Killing Trend," *New York Times,* June 11, 2013). There is a more enduring and perhaps less costly solution. The city that intentionally created high-poverty ghettoes decades ago could atone for its sins and save lives by developing mixed-income communities in the pockets of highest poverty. If Chicago and the nation want troubled youth trapped in high-poverty environs to behave differently, expose them to something else. Give poor families dependent on housing assistance a choice whether to stay or move to a higher-opportunity place, and welcome higher-income people to the neighborhood. With saner public policies, a poor mom could let her kids play outside. A willing, privileged integrationist could live in a diverse neighborhood without fear. And everyone else could begin to move past ghetto stereotypes of black people because there would be fewer places that incubate violent thug life.

77. Sean F. Reardon et al., "Left Behind? The Effect of No Child Left Behind on Academic Achievement Gaps," Stanford University, Center for Education

Policy Analysis (October 5, 2012), 22, http://cepa.stanford.edu/content/left-behind
-effect-no-child-left-behind-academic-achievement-gaps. The effects of NCLB vary
among states and vary inversely with the number of minority students in a school.
But whether a measured impact is positive or negative, generally the impact is very
modest, on the order of changing gaps by 1/100th of a standard deviation per year
on average.

78. Richard Kahlenberg, *Turnaround Schools*.

CHAPTER THREE
Optical Diversity vs. Real Inclusion

1. Anthony P. Carnevale and Jeff Strohl, "How Increasing College Access is
Increasing Inequality and What to Do about It," in *Rewarding Strivers*, ed. Richard Kahlenburg (New York: Century Foundation Press, 2010), 120, www.tcf.org/
assets/downloads/tcf-CarnevaleStrivers.pdf. Only 36 percent of students who
entered community colleges graduated from them and only 54 percent graduated from nonselective colleges. Individual colleges in this nonselective sector
can have graduation rates as low as 13 percent (ibid., 125–26).

2. Ibid., 129–38.

3. Ibid., 122.

4. William Bowen and Derek Bok, *The Shape of the River: Long-Term Consequences of Considering Race in College and University Admissions* (Princeton,
NJ: Princeton University Press, 1998), cited in Richard D. Kahlenberg, *A Better
Affirmative Action: State Universities that Created Alternatives to Racial Preferences*
(Washington, DC: Century Foundation, 2012), http://tcf.org/assets/downloads/
tcf-abaa.pdf, found that 86 percent of African Americans at selective colleges were
middle or upper class.

5. Shaun R. Harper and Kimberly A. Griffin, "Opportunity Beyond Affirmative Action: How Low-Income and Working-Class Black Male Achievers Access
Highly Selective, High-Cost Colleges and Universities," *Harvard Journal of African American Policy* (2011), isites.harvard.edu/icb/icb.do?keyword=k74757&pageid
=icb.page414102. Harper and Griffin drew conclusions from in-depth interviews
conducted with low-income black male achievers at eighteen highly selective, predominantly white institutions.

6. Ibid.

7. Ibid.

8. Caroline M. Hoxby and Christopher Avery, "The Missing 'One-Offs': The
Hidden Supply of High-Achieving, Low-Income Students" (Washington, DC:
Brookings Institution, 2012), www.brookings.edu/~/media/projects/bpea/spring
%202013/2013a_hoxby.pdf.

9. Catherine B. Hill and Gordon C. Winston, "Low-Income Students and
Highly Selective Private Colleges: Geography, Searching, and Recruiting," *Economics of Education Review* 29, no. 4 (2010), 501, www.sciencedirect.com/science/
article/pii/S0272775710000026.

10. Ibid., including fig. 1.

11. See Hoxby and Avery, "The Missing 'One-Offs'," tables 8, 9, and 10.

12. Ibid., 44.

13. Ibid., 18–20, 27.

14. Ydnimporter [anonymous columnist], "Aid Focus Should Be on Economic Diversity," *Yale Daily News*, April 27, 2006, http://yaledailynews.com/blog/2006/04/27/aid-focus-should-be-on-economic-diversity.

15. Paul Fain ("Class Matters," *Inside Higher Ed*, May 2, 2013, www.insidehighered.com/news/2013/05/02/social-class-influences-where-even-valedictorians-go-college-research-finds) cites research by Alexandria Walton Radford, *Top Student, Top School? How Social Class Shapes Where Valedictorians Go to College* (Chicago: University of Chicago Press, 2013).

16. Caroline M. Hoxby and Sarah Turner, "Informing Students about Their College Options: A Proposal for Broadening the Expanding College Opportunities Project," Brookings Institution, June 26, 2013, www.brookings.edu/research/papers/2013/06/26-expanding-college-opportunities-hoxby-turner.

17. Hoxby and Avery, *The Missing 'One-Offs,'* table 7.

18. Hoxby and Avery defined "high-achieving" students as those who score at or above the 90th percentile on the ACT (29 or higher) or SAT I (1300 combined math and verbal) and have a high school grade point average of A- or higher. Black students comprised only 1.5 percent of the national pool that met this threshold, although 5.7 percent of low-income students who met it were black. (For what it's worth, I was a co-valedictorian of my high school with a 4.0 GPA, but my combined SAT score was 1260 on the second try, and my ACT score was 27 on the second try. I would not have been deemed "high achieving" by Hoxby and Avery, but I went on to graduate summa cum laude from Vanderbilt's School of Engineering, making only one B in four years. I challenge the use and meaning of standardized tests in detail in chapter 4.)

19. "News and Views: African Immigrants in the United States are the Nation's Most Highly Educated Group," *Journal of Blacks in Higher Education* 26, no. 60 (January 31, 2000): 60.

20. Sam Roberts, "Out of Africa," *New York Times Upfront* and *Scholastic*, 139, no. 6 (2006), http://teacher.scholastic.com/scholasticnews/indepth/upfront/features/index.asp?article=f112706_out_of_africa.

21. Ibid.; Scott Jaschik, "The Immigrant Factor," *Inside Higher Ed*, February 1, 2007, www.insidehighered.com/news/2007/02/01/black; Jamaica (20.5 percent) and Nigeria (17.3 percent) are the largest feeder countries.

22. Douglas Massey et al., "Black Immigrants and Black Natives Attending Selective Colleges and Universities in the United States," *American Journal of Education* 113 (2007): 243–71, www.umich.edu/~abpafs/blackimmgrants.pdf. In one analysis, immigrant black students had only slightly higher GPAs and took slightly more AP courses than non-immigrant blacks, but they had a statistically significant advantage on SAT scores (average of 1250 compared to 1193).

23. Ibid.

24. Ibid.

25. Samantha Friedman and Emily Rosenbaum, "Does Suburban Residence Mean Better Neighborhood Conditions for All Households? Assessing the Influence of Nativity, Status and Race/Ethnicity," *Social Science Research* 36 (2007): 22.

26. Massey et al., "Black Immigrants and Black Natives"; among black students, 70 percent of immigrants' fathers were college graduates compared to 55 percent of other black students, and 44 percent of immigrant students' fathers had advanced degrees, compared to one-quarter of non-immigrant black students.

27. Pamela R. Bennett and Amy Lutz, "How African American Is the Net Black Advantage? Differences in College Attendance among Immigrant Blacks, Native Blacks, and Whites," *Sociology of Education* 82, no. 1 (January 2009): 70–100, http://soe.sagepub.com/content/82/1/70.short.

28. I explore this idea more fully in chapter 4.

29. Kevin J. A. Thomas, "Race and School Enrollment Among the Children of African Immigrants in the United States," *International Migration Review* (Spring 2012), http://onlinelibrary.wiley.com/doi/10.1111/j.1747-7379.2012.00880.x/abstract.

30. See Sara Rimer and Karen W. Arenson, "Top Colleges Take More Blacks, but Which Ones?" *New York Times*, June 24, 2004, www.nytimes.com/2004/06/24/us/top-colleges-take-more-blacks-but-which-ones.html?pagewanted=all&src=pm.

31. Jane's explanation was more prosaic. The African immigrants who come to America legally negotiate a difficult and lengthy visa application process that itself confers a great deal of economic literacy. To obtain the brass ring of a permanent visa, they must understand how the US economic system works and have a realistic sense of their assets and how they will make a living once here. Upon arriving, they assiduously avoid anyone or anything that might risk this hard-won status. According to Jane, it is a risk aversion that applies to all aspects of life. In my interview with her, she said of this mindset: "I won't go to a club. I won't socialize. I won't enter into relationships. I will avoid anything that could involve losing a job or criminal activity."

32. Rimer and Arenson, "Top Colleges Take More Blacks."

33. See, for example, Jerome Karabel, *The Chosen: The Hidden History of Admission and Exclusion at Harvard, Yale, and Princeton* (Boston: Houghton Mifflin, 2005), 533–34, which describes this practice generally and offers the case example of Princeton's aggressive use of its wealth in the early 2000s to raise its yield with accepted students and best its chief rivals, Yale and Harvard, in the *US News* rankings.

34. Christopher Avery, Andrew Fairbanks, and Richard Zeckhauser, *The Early Admissions Game: Joining the Elite* (Cambridge, MA: Harvard University Press, 2004).

35. Karabel, *The Chosen*, 266; Catherine B. Hill, "Improving Socioeconomic Diversity at Top Colleges and Universities," *Huffington Post*, April 5, 2013, www.huffingtonpost.com/catharine-hill/improving-socioeconomic-d_b_3015590.html.

36. Jennie H. Woo and Susan P. Choy, "Merit Aid for Undergraduates: Trends From 1995–96 to 2007–08," National Center for Education Statistics (October

2011): 9, fig. 4, http://nces.ed.gov/pubs2012/2012160.pdf. In the same period, the percentage of students receiving merit aid at public four-year institutions rose from 8 percent to 18 percent, more than the 16 percent of students who received financial aid in 2007–08.

37. Ibid., 11, fig. 6.

38. Ronald G. Ehrenberg et al., "Crafting a Class: The Trade Off Between Merit Scholarships and Enrolling Lower-Income Students," *Review of Higher Education* 29, no. 2 (Winter 2006): 195–211. The magnitude of this relationship was largest at the institutions that enroll the greatest number of National Merit students.

39. Amanda L. Griffith, "Keeping Up with the Joneses: Institutional Changes Following the Adoption of a Merit Aid Policy," *Economics of Education Review* 30, no. 5 (October 2011): 1022–33.

40. Hill and Winston, "Low-Income Students." Between 2001–2 and 2008–9, the share of students from the bottom 40 percent of family income rose from 10 percent to 11 percent, while the share of students in the top quintile of eligible family income rose from 14.5 percent to 18 percent.

41. Stephen Burd, "Undermining Pell: How Colleges Compete for Wealthy Students and Leave the Low-Income Behind," New America Foundation (May 2013), www.newamerica.net/sites/newamerica.net/files/policydocs/Merit_Aid %20Final.pdf.

42. David L. Sjoquist and John V. Winters, "State Merit-Based Financial Aid Programs and College Attainment," Institute for the Study of Labor (August 2012), http://ftp.iza.org/dp6801.pdf.

43. National Center for Education Statistics, 2007, table 2.

44. Ross Rubenstein and Benjamin Scafidi, "Who Pays and Who Benefits: Examining the Distributional Consequences of the Georgia Lottery for Education," *National Tax Journal* 55, no. 2 (June 2002), http://walkerd.people.cofc .edu/360/AcademicArticles/Scafidi_HOPE.pdf.

45. Christopher Cornwell and David B. Mustard, "Merit-Based College Scholarships and Car Sales," *Education Finance and Policy* 2 (2007): 133–51, http://www .mitpressjournals.org/doi/pdf/10.1162/edfp.2007.2.2.133.

46. Donald E. Heller and Patricia Farrell, "State Merit Scholarship Programs and Racial Inequality," Civil Rights Project, January 1, 2004, http://civilrightsproject .ucla.edu/research/college-access/financing/state-merit-scholarship-programs-and -racial-inequality.

47. Ibid.

48. Nicholas Hillman, "Economic Diversity Among Selective Colleges: Measuring the Enrollment Impact of 'No-Loan' Programs," Institute for Higher Education Policy, 2012, www.ihep.org/assets/files/publications/a-f/(Brief) Economic_Diversity_Among_Selective_Colleges_August_2012.pdf.

49. Hill and Winston, "Low-Income Students," 498.

50. Scott Jaschik, "Dartmouth Drops 'No Loans,'" *Inside Higher Ed*, February 9, 2010, www.insidehighered.com/news/2010/02/09/dartmouth; Kevin Kiley,

"Need Too Much," *Inside Higher Ed*, June 1, 2012, www.insidehighered.com/news/
2012/06/01/wesleyan-shifts-away-need-blind-policy-citing-financial-and-ethical
-concerns; Scott Jaschik, "No Loans Revisited," *Inside Higher Ed*, July 6, 2012,
www.insidehighered.com/news/2012/07/06/cornell-restores-loans-those-family
-incomes-above-60000.

51. Scott Jaschik, "The Cost of Need-Blind," *Inside Higher Ed*, 2013, www
.insidehighered.com/news/2013/02/25/grinnell-will-stay-need-blind-seek-more
-students-ability-pay.

52. Hill, "Improving Socioeconomic Diversity."

53. *US News* Staff, "Best Colleges 2014: About the Rankings/Methodology," *US
News & World Report*, 2013, www.usnews.com/education/best-colleges/articles/
2012/09/11/best-colleges-2013-about-the-rankings-methodology.

54. Lois Lee, "Penn Community Addresses Economic Diversity," *Daily Penn-
sylvanian*, November 24, 2011, www.thedp.com/index.php/article/2011/11/faculty
_students_address_penns_economic_diversity.

55. "SAT/ACT Optional 4-Year Universities," *FairTest*, Fall 2013, www.fairtest
.org/university/optional. In an April 2013 op-ed, Hill stated that a group of presidents of liberal arts colleges were in discussions about reallocating merit aid to
need-based aid. Hill, "Improving Socioeconomic Diversity."

CHAPTER FOUR
Place, Not Race, and Other Radical Reforms

1. "Economic Diversity: National Universities," *US News & World Report*,
http://colleges.usnews.rankingsandreviews.com/best-colleges/rankings/national
-universities/economic-diversity?src=stats&int=4f0116.

2. Anthony P. Carnevale and Jeff Strohl, "How Increasing College Access Is
Increasing Inequality and What to Do about It," in *Rewarding Strivers: Helping
Low-Income Students Succeed in College*, ed. Richard Kahlenberg (New York:
Century Foundation Press, 2010), 136–37, www.tcf.org/assets/downloads/tcf
-CarnevaleStrivers.pdf.

3. "Economic Diversity Among the Top 25 Ranked Schools," *US News and
World Report*, 2013, http://colleges.usnews.rankingsandreviews.com/best-colleges/
rankings/national-universities/economic-diversity-among-top-ranked-schools?src
=stats&int=4f0116.

4. Parker said that a school should be prepared to sacrifice thirty composite
SAT points if you include the writing section in this calculus.

5. Frank L. Samson, "Altering Public University Admission Standards to Preserve White Group Position in the United States," *Comparative Education Review*
57, no. 3 (August 2013): 369–96, www.jstor.org/stable/10.1086/670664.

6. Catherine Rampell, "SAT Scores and Family Income," August 27, 2009,
New York Times, http://economix.blogs.nytimes.com/2009/08/27/sat-scores-and
-family-income.

7. Ibid. See the fourth chart, "All Test Scores."

8. Sean F. Reardon, "The Widening Academic Achievement Gap Between the Rich and the Poor: New Evidence and Possible Explanations," in *Whither Opportunity? Rising Inequality and the Uncertain Life Chances of Low-Income Children*, ed. Greg J. Duncan and Richard J. Murnane (New York: Russell Sage Foundation Press, 2011), http://cepa.stanford.edu/sites/default/files/reardon %20whither%20opportunity%20-%20chapter%205.pdf.

9. Sabino Kornrich and Frank Furstenberg, "Investing in Children: Changes in Parental Spending on Children, 1972 to 2007," *Demography* 50, no. 1 (2012), http://paa2011.princeton.edu/papers/110077.

10. Betty Hart and Todd R. Risley, "The Early Catastrophe: The 30 Million Word Gap," *American Educator* 27, no. 1 (2003), http://www.aft.org/newspubs/periodicals/ae/spring2003/hart.cfm.

11. Mark M. Kishiyama et al., "Socioeconomic Disparities Affect Prefrontal Function in Children," *Journal of Cognitive Neuroscience* 21, no. 6 (2009): 1106–15, http://knightlab.berkeley.edu/statics/publications/2011/06/06/Mark_K_JOCN _2009.pdf.

12. Carnevale and Strohl, "How Increasing College Access Is Increasing Inequality and What to Do about It," 109.

13. Audrey Devine-Eller, "Timing Matters: Test Preparation, Race and Grade Level," *Sociological Forum* 27, no. 2 (June 2012): 458–80, citing research by Kendra Hamilton, http://onlinelibrary.wiley.com/doi/10.1111/j.1573–7861.2012 .01326.x/abstract. A student with a parent actively involved at her school is also more likely to find out about and take advantage of test preparation opportunities.

14. See, generally, Jaesung Choi, "Private Tutoring and Educational Inequality: Evidence from a Dynamic Model of Academic Achievement in Korea," Population Association of America, December 25, 2012, http://paa2013 .princeton.edu/papers/130384; Mark Bray, "Shadow Education: Comparative Perspectives on the Expansion and Implications of Private Supplementary Tutoring," *Procedia Social and Behavioral Sciences* 77, no. 22 (April 2013): 412–20, www .sciencedirect.com/science/article/pii/S1877042813005338.

15. Lani Guinier, "Confirmative Action," *Law and Social Inquiry* 25 (2000): 568, n.9, citing David K. Shipler, "My Equal Opportunity, Your Free Lunch," *New York Times*, March 5, 1995.

16. Ibid. at 565, citing Richard O. Lempert, David A. Chambers, and Terry K. Adams, "Michigan's Minority Graduates in Practice: The River Runs Through Law School," *Law and Social Inquiry* 25 (2000): 395–505.

17. See Saul Geiser and Maria Veronica Santelices, "Validity of High School Grades in Predicting Student Success Beyond the Freshman Year: High School Record vs. Standardized Tests as Indicators of Four-Year College Outcomes," University of California, Berkeley, Center for Studies in Higher Education, 2007, http:// cshe.berkeley.edu/publications/docs/ROPS.GEISER._SAT_6.13.07.pdf.

18. Douglass S. Massey and LiErin Probasco, "Divergent Streams: Race-Gender Achievement Gaps at Selective Colleges and Universities," *Du Bois Review* 7 (2010): 219–46, 241, 244.

19. Carnevale and Strohl, "How Increasing College Access Is Increasing Inequality and What to Do about It," 110.

20. See "Undergraduate Work Team of the Study Group on University Diversity: Recommendations and Observations," University of California, Undergraduate Diversity Work Team, September 2007: 28–36, http://diversity.universityofcalifornia.edu/documents/07-diversity_report.pdf.

21. Richard Perez-Pena, "To Enroll More Minority Students, Colleges Work Around the Courts," *New York Times*, April 1, 2012, www.nytimes.com/2012/04/02/us/college-affirmative-action-policies-change-with-laws.html?pagewanted=all. The University of California system has also greatly expanded programs to identify and cultivate outstanding low-income students, and spends $7 million a year on such programs. Richard Perez-Pena, "In California, Push for College Diversity Starts Earlier," *New York Times*, May 7, 2013, www.nytimes.com/2013/05/08/education/in-california-diversity-in-college-starts-earlier.html?pagewanted=all.

22. See generally, the College Board, "Best Practices in Admissions Decisions," February 1, 2002, http://research.collegeboard.org/sites/default/files/publications/2012/7/misc2002-1-best-practices-admissions-decisions.pdf; "Undergraduate Work Team," University of California, 2007.

23. Carnevale and Strohl, "How Increasing College Access Is Increasing Inequality and What to Do about It," 109.

24. Ibid., 110–11.

25. Erkki Aho et al., *Policy Development and Reform Principles of Basic and Secondary Education in Finland since 1968*, World Bank, May 2006, http://siteresources.worldbank.org/EDUCATION/Resources/278200–1099079877269/547664–1099079967208/Education_in_Finland_May06.pdf.

26. Tamar Lewin, "Testing, Testing: More Students are Taking Both the SAT and ACT," *New York Times*, August 2, 2013, www.nytimes.com/2013/08/04/education/edlife/more-students-are-taking-both-the-act-and-sat.html?pagewanted=all&_r=0.

27. Christine Farr, "After Five Suicides, Palo Alto High School Students Change Culture through Peer Support," January 4, 2011, *Peninsula (CA) Press*, http://peninsulapress.com/2011/01/04/after-five-suicides-palo-alto-high-school-students-change-culture-through-peer-support; "Children and Adolescents and Depression Fact Sheet," National Alliance on Mental Illness, www.nami.org/Template.cfm?Section=Depression&Template=/ContentManagement/ContentDisplay.cfm&ContentID=89198.

28. Lilliana Garces, "The Impact of Affirmative Action Bans in Graduate Education," Civil Rights Project, July 17, 2012, http://civilrightsproject.ucla.edu/research/college-access/affirmative-action/the-impact-of-affirmative-action-bans-in-graduate-education.

29. Ibid., 8.

30. Ibid.

31. Richard Kahlenberg and Halley Potter, "A Better Affirmative Action: State Universities that Created Alternatives to Racial Preferences," Century Foundation, October 3, 2012, 18, http://tcf.org/assets/downloads/tcf-abaa.pdf.

32. Ibid.

33. Ibid.

34. William Julius Wilson, "Race and Affirming Opportunity in the Barack Obama Era," *Du Bois Review: Social Science Research on Race* 9, no. 1 (June 2012): 7–9, doi: 10.1017/51742058x12000240.

35. Kahlenberg and Potter, "A Better Affirmative Action," 16.

36. Ibid., 12.

37. "Undergraduate Work Team of the Study Group on University Diversity: Recommendations and Observations," University of California, Undergraduate Diversity Work Team, September 2007, http://diversity.universityofcalifornia .edu/documents/07-diversity_report.pdf.

38. Transcript of Oral Argument at 42–43, Fisher v. University of Texas at Austin, 132 S. Ct. 1536 (2012) (No. 11–345).

39. Ibid., 43.

40. Randall Kennedy, *For Discrimination: Race, Affirmative Action, and the Law* (New York: Pantheon, 2013), 86 ("the power, wealth, connections, and prestige that accrue to the talented tenth will be shared with non-elite minorities"), 94. Kennedy may view my proposed reform of focusing on place as "an example of race-conscious, class-focused redistribution with racial indicia erased from its exterior." He argues that such strategies will not save affirmative action from white backlash because "one can expect" any program that benefits racial minorities disproportionately "to be attacked as racial affirmative action in disguise" (ibid., 92–93). My explicit agenda, however, is not to help racial minorities by stealth but to help people of all colors who are locked out by unfair structural barriers. Place-based reforms that offer genuine opportunity to people previously shut out have not engendered racial division. Abigail Fisher and her lawyers did not attack the Texas Ten Percent plan and, as I show in chapter 5, a multiracial coalition of supporters and beneficiaries of the plan emerged to defend it from assaults by residents and legislators from affluent school districts.

41. Anthony P. Carnevale and Jeff Strohl, "White Flight Goes to College," *Poverty & Race* 22, no. 5 (September/October 2013): 13, www.prrac.org/pdf/ SeptOct2013Carnevale_Strohl.pdf.

42. See Kahlenberg and Potter, "A Better Affirmative Action."

43. Ibid., 52.

44. "Undergraduate Work Team of the Study Group on University Diversity: Recommendations and Observations," University of California, Undergraduate Diversity Work Team, September 2007, http://diversity.universityofcalifornia.edu/ documents/07-diversity_report.pdf.

45. See Cashin, *Failures of Integration*, 83–126, reviewing this history.

46. "SAT/ACT Optional 4-Year Universities: Test Score Optional List," *FairTest*, www.fairtest.org/university/optional.

47. See the College Board, "The SAT Report on College and Career Readiness: 2012," 2012, 29, http://media.collegeboard.com/homeOrg/content/pdf/sat -report-college-career-readiness-2012.pdf.

48. Lani Guinier, "Colleges Should Take 'Confirmative Action' in Admissions," *Chronicle of Higher Education*, December 14, 2001, http://chronicle.com/article/Colleges-Should-Take/22060.

49. Ibid.

50. Kahlenberg and Potter, "A Better Affirmative Action," citing three polls conducted by the *Los Angeles Times*, EPIC/MRA, and *Newsweek* that show Americans prefer economic to racial affirmative action.

CHAPTER FIVE
Reconciliation

1. Hopwood v. Texas, 78 F.3d 932 (5th Cir. 1996). The *Hopwood* decision was abrogated by the Supreme Court in Grutter v. Bollinger, 539 US 306 (2003), allowing narrowly tailored consideration of race to achieve diversity in higher education.

2. Lani Guinier and Gerald Torres, *The Miner's Canary: Enlisting Race, Resisting Power, Transforming Democracy* (Cambridge, MA: Harvard University Press, 2002), 68–73.

3. See Nicholas Webster, *Analysis of the Texas Ten Percent Plan* (Columbus: Ohio State University, Kirwan Institute for the Study of Race and Ethnicity, 2007), http://kirwaninstitute.osu.edu/reports/2007/08_2007_DemMerit_AnalysisofTXTenPercent.pdf. In 2012, 51 percent of students in the University of Texas system were not white Americans ("University of Texas System, Enrollment Trends by Ethnicity: 2012," in Productivity Dashboard Database, http://exploredata.utsystem.edu).

4. Scott Jaschik, "10% Admissions—The Full Impact," *Inside Higher Ed*, April 6, 2009, www.insidehighered.com/news/2009/04/06/texas, citing research by Mark C. Long et al.

5. Michael A. Olivas, "Don't Scrap Top 10% Plans," *Inside Higher Ed*, April 26, 2007, www.insidehighered.com/views/2007/04/26/olivas. But see Office of Admissions, "Implementation and Results of the Texas Automatic Admissions Law (HB 588) at the University of Texas at Austin," University of Texas at Austin, Office of Admissions, December 23, 2010, www.utexas.edu/student/admissions/research/HB588-Report13.pdf, which shows that median freshman-year grades for ten-percenters and non-ten-percenters have begun to converge at 3.0 at UT Austin.

6. Thurston Domina, "Higher Education Policy as Secondary School Reform: Texas Public High Schools After *Hopwood*," *Educational Evaluation and Policy Analysis* 29, no. 3 (September 2007): 200, 214, http://epa.sagepub.com/content/29/3/200.full.

7. Julie Berry Cullen et al., "Jockeying for Position: Strategic High School Choice under Texas' Top Ten Percent Plan," *Journal of Public Economics* 97 (2013): 32–48, www.sciencedirect.com/science/article/pii/S0047272712000990. See also Kalena E. Cortes and Andrew Friedson, "Ranking Up by Moving Out: The Effect of The Texas Top 10% Plan on Property Values," NBER Working Paper 16663 (2011), National Bureau of Economic Research, www.nber.org/papers/w16663, which

finds evidence of strategic choices to move to neighborhoods with low-performing schools and a simultaneous increases in property values in those neighborhoods.

8. See, generally Cashin, *Failures of Integration,* 202–36, which discusses the disproportionate influence middle-class suburbs possess.

9. David Bacon, "How Mississippi's Black/Brown Strategy Beat the South's Anti-Immigrant Wave," *Nation,* April 20, 2012, www.thenation.com/article/167465/how-mississippis-blackbrown-strategy-beat-souths-anti-immigrant-wave.

10. Ibid.

11. Juan F. Perea et al., *Race and Races: Cases and Resources for a Diverse America* (St. Paul, MN: West Group, 2007), 102–3, which cites Edmund S. Morgan's 1975 *American Slavery, American Freedom* (New York: Norton, 1975), 327–28.

12. Susan Eaton, "Black-Latino Coalitions Block Anti-Immigrant Laws in Mississippi," *Autumn Awakening* 18, no. 2 (2011), www.urbanhabitat.org/18-2/eaton.

13. Bacon, "How Mississippi's Black/Brown Strategy Beat the South's Anti-Immigrant Wave."

14. Eaton, "Black-Latino Coalitions Block Anti-Immigrant Laws in Mississippi."

15. Ibid.

16. Bacon, "How Mississippi's Black/Brown Strategy Beat the South's Anti-Immigrant Wave."

17. Richard Fausset, "Tough Anti-Illegal-Immigration Law Dies in Mississippi," *Los Angeles Times,* April 3, 2012, http://articles.latimes.com/2012/apr/03/nation/la-na-nn-mississippi-immigration-20120403.

18. Bacon, "How Mississippi's Black/Brown Strategy Beat the South's Anti-Immigrant Wave."

19. This slogan comes from a MIRA flyer about Civic Engagement Day inserted in MIRA's October-December 2012 newsletter; Mississippi Immigrant Rights Alliance, "Come Join Us on Civic Engagement Day: Support Human Rights for All" (2012), 4, www.yourmira.org/media/uploads/2013/03/MIRA_OCT_NOV_DEC_20120001.pdf.

20. MIRA's October-December 2012 newsletter (2012), 5, www.yourmira.org/media/uploads/2013/03/MIRA_OCT_NOV_DEC_20120001.pdf.

21. Stokely Carmichael and Charles V. Hamilton, *Black Power: The Politics of Liberation in America* (New York: Vintage, 1967), 75.

22. Paul Osterman, *Gathering Power: The Future of Progressive Politics in America* (Boston: Beacon, 2002), 67.

23. Ibid., 42–47, 51, 67, 93, 185.

24. *Health Insurance Coverage of the Total Population,* Kaiser Family Foundation, 2011, http://kff.org/other/state-indicator/total-population.

25. William Julius Wilson, *The Bridge Over the Racial Divide: Rising Inequality and Coalition Politics* (Berkeley: University of California Press, 1999), 85–92.

26. Paul Osterman, *Gathering Power,* 75–81.

27. Chambers of commerce from Dallas, San Antonio, and elsewhere that normally align with Governor Perry lobbied in support of Medicaid expansion along with many hospitals because of the beneficial economics that would flow from increased federal funds. David Mildenberg, "Chambers get behind Medicaid," *Star-Telegram*, March 19, 2013, http://www.star-telegram.com/2013/03/18/4712409/chambers-get-behind-medicaid.html?rh=1. As of the fall of 2013, Texas had not opted to change Medicaid eligibility pursuant to the Affordable Care Act.

28. Wilson, *The Bridge Over the Racial Divide*, 115.

29. Lani Guinier and Gerald Torres, *The Miner's Canary*.

30. See, for example, Philip Mazzocco, *The Dangers of Not Speaking About Race*, Kirwan Institute for the Study of Race and Ethnicity, 2006, 6, www.kirwaninstitute.osu.edu/reports/2006/05_2006_DangersofNotTalkingAboutRace.pdf; Maya Wiley et al., *Why We Must Talk About Race to Win Better Policy*, Center for Social Inclusion, 2010, www.centerforsocialinclusion.org/files/2010/03/CSI-Talking-Effectively-About-Race-and-Policy-in-an-Obama-Era.pdf.

31. Jennifer L. Knight and Michelle R. Hebl, "Affirmative Reaction: The Influence of Type of Justification on Non-Beneficiary Attitudes towards Affirmative-Action Plans in Higher Education," *Journal of Social Issues* 3, no. 61 (2005): 547, http://onlinelibrary.wiley.com/doi/10.1111/j.1540-4560.2005.00420.x/abstract. For example, a study that tested white college students' reactions to affirmative action for their school found that those who received a justification based upon the advantages of diversity were less supportive than those who received explanations about the need to address past racial discrimination. But as I suggest in previous chapters, racial resentments around race-based affirmative action are best dealt with not through better messaging but through reforms that help all disadvantaged people.

32. john a. powell and Rachel Godsil, "Implicit Bias Insights as Preconditions to Structural Change," *Poverty and Race* 20, no. 5 (2011): 6, www.prrac.org/full_text.php?text_id=1363&item_id=13241&newsletter_id=119&header=Race+%2F+Racism&kc=1.

33. "Racialization" refers to "the set of practices, cultural norms and institutional arrangements that both reflect and help to create and maintain [racialized] outcomes in society" (john a. powell, *Racing to Justice: Transforming Our Conception of Self and Other to Build an Inclusive Society* [Bloomington: Indiana University Press, 2012], 4). *Racism* implies a consciously motivated force, while *racialization* implies "a process or set of processes that may or may not be animated by conscious forces" (john a. powell, "Deepening Our Understanding of Structural Marginalization," *Poverty and Race* 22, no. 5 [September/October 2013]: 3, www.prrac.org/pdf/SeptOct2013PRRAC_powell.pdf).

34. See Cashin, *Failures of Integration,* 202–36, which surveys the costs to whites of racial and economic segregation.

35. The late Manning Marable argued, for example, that organizing around racial identity invites zero-sum politics; see Manning Marable, "Building Coalitions among Communities of Color: Beyond Identity Politics," in *Blacks,*

Latinos, and Asians in Urban America, ed. James Jennings (Westport, CT: Praeger Publishers, 1994).

36. Rachel Godsil, "A Multiplicity of Interests," *Columbia Journal of Race and Law* Special Feature 2, no. 9 (2012): 12, which cites Samuel R. Sommers and Phoebe C. Ellsworth, "White Juror Bias: An Investigation of Prejudice Against Black Defendants in the Courtroom," *Psychology, Public Policy, and Law* 7 (2001), finding that "many Whites embrace an egalitarian value system and desire to appear non-prejudiced"; Alexander R. Green et al., "Implicit Bias Among Physicians and Its Prediction of Thrombolysis Decisions for Black and White Patients," *Journal of General Internal Medicine* 22 (2007), http://link.springer.com/article/10.1007 %2Fs11606-007-0258-5#page-1, which finds that "those physicians who were aware that the study had to do with racial bias, and who had higher levels of implicit pro-white bias, were more likely to recommend thrombolysis to black patients than physicians with low bias."

37. powell and Godsil, "Implicit Bias Insights as Preconditions to Structural Change," 6; Godsil, "A Multiplicity of Interests," 13; powell, "Deepening Our Understanding of Structural Marginalization," 3.

38. Godsil, "A Multiplicity of Interests," 13, which cites Linda R. Tropp and Rebecca A. Bianchi, "Valuing Diversity and Interest in Interest Group Contact," *Journal of Social Issues* 62 (2006); J. Nicole Shelton and Jennifer A. Richeson, "Pluralistic Ignorance and Intergroup Contact," *Journal of Personality and Social Psychology* 88 (2005); E. Ashby Plant and Patricia G. Devine, "Interracial Interactions: Approach and Avoidance," in *Handbook of Approach and Avoidance Motivation*, ed. Andrew J. Elliot (New York: Psychology Press, 2008), 571.

39. See, for example, Pema Levy, "Obamacare Shutdown Fight: Ted Cruz Helped His Supporters Raise Money By Hurting Fellow Republicans," *International Business Times*, September 20, 2013, www.ibtimes.com/obamacare -shutdown-fight-ted-cruz-helped-his-supporters-raise-money-hurting-fellow -republicans.

40. Full disclosure: the author of this book currently serves as vice chair of the board of Building One America.

41. Sheryll Cashin, "Shall We Overcome? 'Post Racialism' and Inclusion in the 21st Century," *Alabama Civil Rights and Civil Liberties Law Review* 31 (2011): 46–47.

42. Associated Press, "NJ Affordable Housing Revamp Weighed," *Times Herald-Record*, May 22, 2008, www.recordonline.com/apps/pbcs.dll/article?AID =/20080522/BIZ/805222021/-1/rss06.

43. Myron Orfield and Thomas Luce, "America's Racially Diverse Suburbs," 3, citing Myron Orfield, *American Metropolitics: The New Suburban Reality* (Washington, DC: Brookings Institution, 2002), 155–72.

44. "Americans Say They Like Diverse Communities; Election, Census Trends Suggest Otherwise," Pew Research Center, December 2, 2008, www.pewsocialtrends .org/2008/12/02/americans-say-they-like-diverse-communities-election-census -trends-suggest-otherwise.

45. Meghan A. Burke. "Diversity and Its Discontents: Ambivalence in Neighborhood Policy and Racial Attitudes in the Obama Era," *Journal of Race and Policy* 6, no. 1 (2010): 80–94, http://works.bepress.com/meghan_burke/4.

46. Robert D. Putnam and Lewis M. Feldstein, "Politics and Government," in *Better Together* (Cambridge, MA: John F. Kennedy School of Government, 2001), http://bettertogether.org/pdfs/Politics.pdf.

47. Raj Chetty et al., The Equality of Opportunity Project, http://www.equality-of-opportunity.org.

48. Susan Eaton, "Black-Latino Coalitions Block Anti-Immigrant Laws in Mississippi," *Autumn Awakening* 18, no. 2 (2011): 38, www.urbanhabitat.org/18-2/eaton.

49. Martin Luther King Jr., "Letter from Birmingham Jail," in *Why We Can't Wait* (New York: Harper & Row, 1964), 77–100.

50. For an incisive analysis of the overuse of racial disparities, see john a. powell, "Deepening Our Understanding of Structural Marginalization."

51. Thomas Edsall, "The Reproduction of Privilege," *New York Times*, March 12, 2012, http://campaignstops.blogs.nytimes.com/2012/03/12/the-reproduction-of-privilege.

52. Paul Osterman, *Gathering Power*, 16–17, 21.

53. Steven Greenhouse, "Labor Unions Claim Credit for Obama's Victory," *New York Times*, November 7, 2012, http://thecaucus.blogs.nytimes.com/2012/11/07/labor-unions-claim-credit-for-obamas-victory; see also David Madland and Nick Bunker, "Unions Make Democracy Work for the Middle Class," Center for American Progress, American Worker Project, 2012, www.americanprogressaction.org/issues/labor/report/2012/01/25/10913/unions-make-democracy-work-for-the-middle-class.

54. John R. Logan and Wenquan Zhang, "Global Neighborhoods: New Evidence from Census 2010," US2010 Project (November 2011), which describes global neighborhoods as those where the "traditional black-white color line is replaced by a more complex array of whites, blacks, Hispanics, and Asians" in substantial numbers, www.s4brown.edu/us2010/data/Report/globalfinal2.pdf; Orfield and Luce, "America's Racially Diverse Suburbs," 2, 8, which notes that in 2010, almost one-third of the population in the fifty-largest metropolitan areas—nearly 53 million people—lived in diverse suburbs that were 20–60 percent non-white.

55. US Department of Health and Human Services, "Adoption USA: A Chart Book Based on the 2007 National Survey of Adoptive Parents," http://aspe.hhs.gov/hsp/09/nsap/chartbook/index.cfm.

56. Pew Research Center, "The Rise of Intermarriage: Rates, Characteristics Vary by Race and Gender," February 16, 2012, www.pewsocialtrends.org/files/2012/02/SDT-Intermarriage-II.pdf. Nearly all young adults born after 1980 say they are "fine" with interracial marriage, and 85 percent are personally open to marrying someone of any other racial group. Pew Research Center, "Almost All Millennials Accept Interracial Dating and Marriage," February 1, 2010, www.pewresearch.org/2010/02/01/almost-all-millennials-accept-interracial-dating-and-marriage.

Most millennials also have friends of a different race. Among white millennials, 56 percent have black friends, compared to just 36 percent of whites ages fifty to sixty-four. "Blacks Upbeat about Black Progress, Prospects A Year After Obama's Election," Pew Research Social and Demographic Trends, January 12, 2010, www .pewsocialtrends.org/2010/01/12/blacks-upbeat-about-black-progress-prospects.

57. Amanda B. Brodish, "More Eyes on the Prize: Variability in White Americans' Perceptions of Progress Toward Racial Equality," *Personality and Social Psychology Bulletin* 34, no. 4 (2008): 513–27.

58. Christopher L. Aberson et al., "Implicit Bias and Contact: The Role of Interethnic Friendships," *Journal of Social Psychology* 144, no. 3 (2004): 335–47.

59. Paul Osterman, *Gathering Power*, 18–20, 53–54; Devon W. Carbado and Donald Weiss, *Time On Two Crosses: The Collected Writings of Bayard Rustin* (San Francisco: Gleis Press, 2003), xxiv.

CONCLUSION

1. James Madison, "Federalist No. 10," in *The Federalist Papers*, http://thomas .loc.gov/home/histdox/fed_10.html.

2. Frederick Douglass, "The Dred Scott Decision," speech, New York, May 11, 1857, University of Rochester Fredrick Douglass Project, www.lib.rochester.edu/ index.cfm?PAGE=4399.

3. Prerna Anand, "Winners and Losers: Corrections and Higher Education in California," *California Common Sense*, September 5, 2012, www.cacs.org/ca/ article/44; John Fensterwald, "California Drops to 49th in School Spending in Annual Ed Week Report," *EdSource*, January 14, 2013, www.edsource.org/today/2013/ california-drops-to-49th-in-school-spending-in-annual-ed-week-report/25379# .Ul7R8NKsjTo.